S0-ABB-549

Zealous for the Truth

Zealous for the Truth

2 Peter, 2 & 3 John, Jude

This inductive Bible study is designed for individual, small group, or classroom use. A leader's guide with full lesson plans and the answers to the Bible study questions is available from Regular Baptist Press. Order RBP0051 online at www.regularbaptistpress.org, e-mail orders@rbpstore.org, call toll-free 1-800-727-4440, or contact your distributor.

REGULAR BAPTIST PRESS
1300 North Meacham Road
Schaumburg, Illinois 60173-4806

The Doctrinal Basis of Our Curriculum

A more detailed statement with references is available upon request.

- The verbal, plenary inspiration of the Scriptures
- Only one true God
- The Trinity of the Godhead
- The Holy Spirit and His ministry
- The personality of Satan
- The Genesis account of creation
- Original sin and the fall of man
- The virgin birth of Christ
- Salvation through faith in the shed blood of Christ
- The bodily resurrection and priesthood of Christ
- Grace and the new birth
- Justification by faith
- Sanctification of the believer
- The security of the believer
- The church
- The ordinances of the local church: baptism by immersion and the Lord's Supper
- Biblical separation— ecclesiastical and personal
- Obedience to civil government
- The place of Israel
- The pretribulation rapture of the church
- The premillennial return of Christ
- The millennial reign of Christ
- Eternal glory in Heaven for the righteous
- Eternal torment in Hell for the wicked

ZEALOUS FOR THE TRUTH: 2 PETER, 2 & 3 JOHN, JUDE
Adult Bible Study Book
Vol. 60, No. 1
© 2011
Regular Baptist Press • Schaumburg, Illinois
www.regularbaptistpress.org • 1-800-727-4440
Printed in U.S.A.
All rights reserved
RBP0054 • ISBN: 978-1-60776-487-8

Contents

Preface

What are you zealous for? Your kids, your bank account, your health, the Cubs? Does the *truth* make the initial list that comes to your mind? Have you ever considered the need to be zealous for the truth God carefully conveyed in His Word?

Second Peter, 2 and 3 John, and Jude have a lot to say about being zealous. *Zealous for the Truth* is a study of these four epistles that were written to instruct believers about life during the last days before the rapture of the church. We are living in the last days so these epistles were written with us in mind.

This study emphasizes being zealous for God's Word, living with proper Christian behavior and evangelistic concern, and the importance of identifying and rejecting false teachers. Through studying these epistles, you will understand the need for discernment of truth. The epistles will prompt you to consider how well you know the Bible. And they will encourage you to live as a genuine Christian during these troubled-filled last days.

Enjoy this study. Let these challenging books of the Bible guide you as you consider how your priorities need realigned to fit God's instructions for the church today.

Growing Expectations

*God's power is sufficient for believers as they
strive to be all God wants them to be.*

2 Peter 1:1–7

**"According as his divine power hath given unto
us all things that pertain unto life and godliness,
through the knowledge of him that hath called
us to glory and virtue" (2 Peter 1:3).**

Being zealous for the truth is perhaps hardest for defense lawyers to do. They are sworn to be a zealous advocate for their clients, even those clients who confess to them that they are guilty as charged. A good defense lawyer will be zealous to defend his client without using chicanery to deceive juries concerning witnesses or evidence. But the line between loyalty to clients and ethical behavior is sometimes fuzzy and hard to define. Defense lawyers must decide how to be loyal while remaining ethical.

Believers don't have to struggle with such questions. God calls us to be zealous for the truth and for Him. There is no conflict in such callings. As we defend the truth we are also taking a stand for God.

Getting Started

1. What are you zealous for?

2. Does the *truth* make your initial list? Why or why not?

3. Can you really say you are zealous for anything? Explain.

The books of 2 Peter, 2 and 3 John, and Jude were written to instruct believers about life during the last days before the rapture of the church. These books have a lot to say about zealously defending and living the truth.

Searching the Scriptures

This study will focus on becoming all God wants you to be. Learning about His provisions for your spiritual growth should cause you to be zealous about growing.

Writer and Readers

4. Read 2 Peter 1:1a. Peter calls himself a "servant." Why is that an indicator of spiritual growth in Peter's life?

Peter is both Christ's servant and one of His apostles (2 Peter 1:1). A servant of Christ is ready always to receive and to obey the directives of his Master. Personal humility is combined with apostolic authority in Peter.

Peter takes his place next to the other apostles and not above them. Though he was one of the leaders of the Jerusalem church, Peter refers to himself as "an" apostle and not "the" apostle of Jesus Christ.

The apostles were messengers sent out with orders from Christ with full authority from Him. Their responsibility was to deliver Christ's message, not their own (Galatians 1:11).

5. Read 2 Peter 1:1b. How does this verse dispel the idea that some believers have special privileges from God that account for their ability to grow spiritually?

Peter identifies his readers as those who have received the same precious faith as that of the apostles. While Peter's letter is written first to believers in a certain geographical location, it is written to all of us who embrace the same precious faith. There is no distinction between the apostles and all other Christians. We all have this faith through God's grace. The word "obtained" (v. 1) implies the lack of any merit as the source of the gift.

Our possession of faith is due to God's righteous act of providing the gospel. It is "God and our Saviour Jesus Christ" Who has righteously provided for our salvation.

Greeting

Peter's greeting in verse 2 is more than a typical first-century greeting, for it has doctrinal significance. The apostle desires that grace and peace be multiplied in the lives of God's people. There are no limits to the experience of grace and peace that God has for us. Grace is God's unmerited kindness extended to us. Peace is the inward tranquility that flows from experiencing God's grace.

6. What happens to the believer who seeks peace through a means other than a growing relationship with Christ?

Both grace and peace come to us because we know God (v. 2). This is knowledge that springs from a personal and intimate relationship with Jesus Christ.

Our knowledge of God grows with the study of the Scriptures. As we place our trust continually in His Word and commit ourselves to His purposes, our knowledge of Him becomes more personal. We experience answers to prayer, the evidence of God's working in our lives, and the strengthening of our faith.

Divine Power

7. The United States Army had a recruitment slogan: "Be All That You Can Be." What did this slogan mean in that context?

Christians can be all that God wants them to be. He has supplied us with all the resources necessary to make spiritual growth and maturity possible and practical.

8. Read 2 Peter 1:3. Why are all excuses for not growing as a Christian unreasonable?

God's power is more than adequate for us to live godly. The words "all things" sum up this truth.

Life and godliness merge together in Christian experience (v. 3). A believer is divinely equipped to live a godly life, which is what the Christian life is all about. "Life" is the eternal life that we possess now, which means that we know God within a personal relationship with Him. Respect out of reverence for God is the meaning of "godliness," which all believers are expected to pursue. The moment we came to know God through Jesus Christ, He made His power available to us to live godly lives in fellowship with Him.

9. What might be some clues that a person is trying to live a godly life based on his or her own power instead of God's power?

Peter explains that God called us to this experience for His own glory and virtue (v. 3). God's glory is the sum of all that He is, while His virtue is His moral goodness.

Precious Promises

God has also given His promises to us for His own glory and virtue (v. 4). These promises are beyond our comprehension and precious.

10. Read 2 Peter 1:4. Which of God's promises do you particularly appreciate as you seek to grow spiritually?

God's promises to us include all of God's provisions for our salvation and godly living. What God has promised makes His promises precious to us.

11. Do believers generally value God's promises? Why? Why not?

The purpose for these promises is that we might be sharers in His nature (v. 4). To share God's nature means believers share in certain attributes of God's character. Some of these attributes are mercy, kindness, long-suffering, and forbearance. As a result, we are new creations in Christ (2 Corinthians 5:17). This is not the end of the story though. At the rapture of the church, we will be conformed completely to Christ's likeness (Romans 8:23–29). Can there be any doubt that these promises are great and precious promises?

Our participation in the divine nature is parallel to experiencing eternal life and godliness (2 Peter 1:3). The "all things" that God gives to us for godly living include sharing in some of His attributes.

This transforming experience involves a radical change from what we were to what we have become in Christ (v. 4). It began when we embraced Christ by faith and turned our backs on the moral pollution resident in the world. The change involves a switch from living to satisfy personal desires to seeking to know and fulfill God's desires.

The false teachers with whom Peter takes issue in this letter have not fled from the moral corruption of the world (2:20, 21). Eventually they are snarled and overpowered by it. Their situation illustrates Peter's decisive point (1:4). We began to share in God's nature only after we separated ourselves from the world's moral corruption. The moment we placed our trust in the promises of God and were spiritually renewed, we crossed the point of no return.

12. What can you do to apply the resources for growth to your life?

Faith in God's promises generates a chain of internal and external changes in us. This is what participation in the divine nature is all about.

Faith First

13. Read 2 Peter 1:5–7. Why is faith first in the list of Christian character qualities?

Peter now stresses the Christian's part in the outworking of his or her salvation. This is the meaning of "and beside this." We are to bring along the side of our faith in God those things consistent with godly living. The massive resources of God's power and promises make this possible.

Faith is both foundational and functional. Through the channel of faith, we receive God's grace (Ephesians 2:8, 9). Character development follows. Faith is a virtue itself, but it is also the root of all the other virtues.

Character Qualities

Peter presents a list of Christian character qualities to be added to our faith in Christ. These virtues provide us with a sketch of a true Christian character (2 Peter 1:5–7). There is not a logical flow to Peter's list, except that we must begin with faith.

Peter mentions virtue after faith (v. 5). Virtue is goodness and is an attribute of God. When we behave in a virtuous manner, we reflect God's character.

The next character quality on Peter's list is knowledge (v. 5). Our knowledge of God comes from careful study and meditation on His Word. Adding knowledge is more than accumulating information bites. It is arranging our knowledge of God's Word in a meaningful way. This means that we claim His promises and obey His commands while worshiping, trusting, and relying on Him.

14. How should the virtue of knowledge affect the way we read and study the Bible?

Temperance follows knowledge on the list (v. 6). Temperance is self-control. The word was an athletic term denoting strict discipline. Athletes were expected to abstain from unwholesome food, drink, and sexual indulgence in preparation for their contests. Self-control for the believer is moderation with regard to good things, as well as abstention in all circumstances from unwholesomeness. We exercise self-control with God's provision of divine power for godly living.

15. What happens when we try to exercise self-control by our own power?

Peter adds patience next (v. 6). The word "patience" means "to remain under." Patience is perseverance. It is the character trait of persisting in faith while experiencing the severest of trials and suffering. Patience has its source in faith, because the Christian knows that God is in complete control of every situation.

16. How aware have you been of the connection between patience and trust in God?

17. How does understanding the connection help you be patient in trials and sufferings?

Godliness follows next in the apostle's roster of virtues (v. 6). Godliness is respect and reverence toward God, which springs from a proper relationship with God. It is devotion toward God, which results from faith in God.

18. How would you know a person reverences God?

The last two character qualities in Peter's catalog express love (v. 7). Brotherly kindness is the love that Christians express to each other as brothers in Christ. We are partakers of the divine nature together. The quality of our relationship is demonstrably different from any other human relationship experienced by people.

Love for our brothers in Christ is loyal love. It entails bearing each other's burdens, sorrows, and difficulties. It means that we guard each other from the destructive power of gossip, prejudice, and narrowness, and the refusal to accept a believer for who he is in Christ.

19. What might believers convey about their relationship with God if they are fighting with one another and sinning against one another with their words?

Christian love is not restricted to other Christians (v. 7). Love is a debt that we owe to all men, even our enemies. God models this for us because His love is not evoked by who we are, but by Who He is (John 3:16). So it is not that we are lovable, but instead that God is love. We, therefore, are to be marked by an indiscriminate and deliberate habit of loving those outside the Christian family circle.

Making It Personal

20. What excuses, if any, have you been using for a lack of spiritual growth?

21. What specific truths in 2 Peter 1:1–7 will help you stop making excuses for not growing?

22. What steps will you take to deepen your faith in God's provision for your spiritual growth?

23. When was the last time you praised God for the spiritual growth in your life? Do so today.

24. Memorize 2 Peter 1:3.

Stirring Up Your Memory

Christians should give diligence to make their salvation sure by developing Christian character.

2 Peter 1:8–14

"Wherefore the rather, brethren, give diligence to make your calling and election sure: for if ye do these things, ye shall never fall" (2 Peter 1:10).

Did you ever hear the JIF peanut butter commercial, "Choosey mothers choose JIF!" These choosey mothers were "fastidiously selective, particular." And the makers of JIF wanted their audience to believe that these moms selected JIF because they wanted only the best for their kids. Well, "choosey" can be another word for "picky," which is defined as "fussy" too. Now there's a word! It can mean "requiring or giving close attention to details" (that's pretty good, isn't it?) or "revealing a sometimes extreme concern for niceties" (not so good). Picky people can save the day when their dissatisfaction with less-than-perfect results pays off, or they can just irritate everyone around them.

Getting Started

1. Are you a picky person? What, if anything, are you pickiest about?

2. How is your level of satisfaction with your spiritual growth affected by your pickiness?

3. In what sense should every believer be a little picky about their spiritual growth?

Peter talks about believers' need to grow spiritually. All of us should look at our level of spiritual growth with some measure of dissatisfaction.

Searching the Scriptures

Life of Fruitfulness

In 2 Peter 1, Peter exhorts believers to develop character qualities so they will reap an abundant harvest. If believers neglect these virtues, the results will be spiritual forfeiture and loss. The apostle deals with this possibility positively (v. 8) and then negatively (v. 9).

The positive side of the exhortation is that a continual increase in faith, virtue, knowledge, patience, godliness, brotherly kindness, and charity will lead to an abundant spiritual harvest for us. The thrust of Peter's argument is that we must foster all of these character qualities all of the time without any pause. God intends that we take no vacation or leaves of absence; we must give complete attention to being all that we can be for His glory.

4. What happens when a believer tries to take a vacation from spiritual growth?

5. Have you ever tried to take a vacation from growing spiritually? If so, what was the result?

Peter identifies two outcomes for abounding in these character qualities (v. 8). First, believers are not "barren," or ineffective. Here Peter uses a negative statement to make a positive point: we will live godly lives in which we experience and demonstrate the power of God. The fruit of Christian character qualities will be evident in our lives.

6. If a believer's ministry is ineffective because of a lack of his or her spiritual growth, what good will changing the believer's ministry methods do?

The second outcome is that believers will not be "unfruitful," or unproductive (v. 8). Peter again uses a negative statement to present a positive truth: these character traits will be evident in our thinking and behavior, like produce from a fruit tree.

Peter is writing about maturing spiritually. God has created us so we normally grow physically, mentally, and emotionally. Character development is bound up with human development. We believers have an added dimension, the spiritual side of our characters. While it is distinct, it is nonetheless an integral part of our personal identity. People should think of us first as people of Christian character.

7. What three words would those who are closest to you use to describe you?

8. Do any of their three words relate to your Christian character?

Our spiritual maturity begins and continues with knowing Jesus Christ (v. 8). This does not mean simply knowledge, but knowledge that is essential to a relationship. Within this relationship we develop and grow in Christian character.

Certain of Salvation

9. Read 1 Peter 1:9, 10. What is the connection between Christian character development and a believer's spiritual confidence and stability?

Peter explains that believers who abound in Christian virtues see the end of the way (v. 9). Again the apostle uses the negative ("he that lacketh . . . is blind") to express the positive: those who have these things see the ultimate purpose for which they are saved. God will consummate the redemptive work that He began at our salvation by completely conforming us to the image of Christ. Until then God's purpose is that we move toward the goal by continuing to mature spiritually.

The nearsighted believer sees only the present, for his goal is to just get through today without a diligent commitment to spiritual maturity (v. 9). He is absorbed with only those things that are close at hand. He does not look at the goal ahead, and he has forgotten that God cleansed him from his sins for a purpose. Actually, he is living in a "disconnect" with the future and the past.

10. How should remembering Christ's work on the cross affect our spiritual growth?

11. How should considering our future glorification affect our spiritual growth?

Spiritual progress prevents spiritual amnesia. As we progress in maturing in Christian character, we remain aware of our forgiveness and cleansing from sin. We experience the joy of being a new creation in Christ (2 Corinthians 5:17). The Christian who suffers from spiritual amnesia does so because he has forgotten that he has been purged from his sins (2 Peter 1:9). He has failed to make the effort he should in character development (v. 5).

Spiritual myopia and amnesia are progressive unless reversed. Peter calls all of us believers to decisive action, to diligently make our salvation certain (v. 10). We do this by abounding in the effective and fruitful development of Christian character qualities (v. 8). Our godly living provides us with the evidence that we are saved. It, in turn, results in personal assurance.

We cannot make our salvation more certain than it truly is, but we are to make it sure for ourselves in our own hearts and minds. Our growth in Christian character provides us with unmistakable evidence that we are saved.

12. Why is it important to make clear that a believer's spiritual growth gives evidence of his salvation but is not part of his salvation?

Specifically Christians are to make every effort to be sure of their calling and election (v. 10). "Calling" refers to God's effective invitation to sinners to receive His salvation. Our calling is a holy calling, which arose from God's purpose and grace. Our response as believers is to lead lives worthy of our calling (Ephesians 4:1, 2).

"Election" refers to the choice God made before He laid the foundation of the world (2 Peter 1:10). He chose that we should be in Christ (Ephesians 1:5). We thank God that He has chosen us to come to Christ through the work of the Holy Spirit and trust in the gospel. Gratitude, not pride, is the proper response to God's saving grace. Election is neither a throne from which we judge others nor a bed of ease on which we sleep in moral laxity. Election provides us with assurance, especially in dark times of distress. The fruitfulness of Christian character does not produce our election, but fruitfulness is an evidence of our election.

We not only make certain our eternal relationship with God by growth in Christian character, but we are also kept from falling (2 Peter

1:10). Here Peter is referring to stumbling and falling into error, which is the reason he warns about false teachers (2:1, 20–22). Heretical teachings are a peril to our spiritual maturing. Becoming stunted in our growth leads to misery and grief—even to a potential loss of usefulness in Christian ministry (1 Corinthians 9:27).

Peter's admonition in 2 Peter 1:10 does not mean that we will never sin. However, God will never change His mind about us. We will never suffer a reverse, for we cannot lose or forfeit our salvation.

Abundant Entrance

As believers, we anticipate the future earthly kingdom of Christ (v. 11). This kingdom that will last forever is a part of our Christian hope. We are already members of this coming kingdom, and we shall enter it.

In 2 Peter 1:11 the apostle Peter is referring to the manner of our entrance into this kingdom: believers who have an abundance of fruitfulness will have an abundant entrance.

13. Read 2 Peter 1:11. Is the concept of this verse—with its emphasis on the rich quality of our entrance into the presence of God—a new thought for you?

14. How often does a typical believer think about God's positive anticipation for the arrival of a faithful believer?

Repetition of the Facts

As Peter reflects on the present and eternal implications of what he has written, he expresses a resolve: to keep on reminding believers of the importance of spiritual maturity. We always face the danger of being preoccupied with the things of life and of forgetting about the things of eternity. Forgetting God's truth is hazardous to our identity as believers.

15. How has focusing on eternity made a difference in your life?

Peter's commitment to this task is set within the particular circum-stances of his own life and death, as well as within the circumstances that might occur to Christians who survive him.

The Intent of Repeating the Facts

Peter expresses his intent with action words. He intends "to put" be-lievers in remembrance. In verse 13 he intends to stir up their memory. He never forgot the admonition of Christ that he, Peter, was to strength-en fellow believers after his restoration (Luke 22:32).

The apostle intends to remind his readers about "these things" (2 Peter 1:12) in the preceding verses, about the truths we embrace by personal faith. Peter affirms later in this chapter 1 that the truth we be-lieve came to us by special revelation (vv. 20, 21). The apostles are the proclaimers of the truth, not the creators of truth. The same is true of God's people as His witnesses.

We have a solemn reminder that it is all too easy for those who are fixed in the faith to forget (v. 12). Those who forget the truth are in danger of wobbling spiritually. The unstable are moving targets for false teachers (2:14). Those who distort the meaning of Scripture are unstable (3:16).

The Occasion of the Reminder

Peter considers it his "meet," or just, duty to call Christians to re-member the truth (1:13). Reminding his readers is proper, in a judicial sense; it is the right thing to do.

Furthermore, he sees his body as a tent to be taken down (v. 13). So he is determined to make the best use of the remaining time allotted to him. A tent is a temporary dwelling pitched for a short time. While God allows us to enjoy the property, we must use it as something that really belongs to Him (1 Corinthians 6:20).

16. How might a believer affect his spiritual growth by viewing his body as a "permanent dwelling" instead of a tent?

Peter's purpose is to arouse thoroughly, or to "stir," the minds of God's people (2 Peter 1:13). The word "stir" was used of arousing a person from drowsy inattention. Peter's readers need a refresher course in what they know.

Peter speaks of his forthcoming demise very calmly (v. 14). Death is an exodus from this world and an entrance into God's presence. He has no fear of death, for he knows he will move to a new, far better location. This is God's will for him. He has lived for years in the knowledge of a horrible and painful death. Nonetheless he speaks of it without fear or regret.

17. How might focusing on spiritual growth affect the amount of fear we have as we face death?

Making It Personal

18. How confident and stable have you been as a believer?

19. How might a renewed focus on spiritual growth in your life change your level of confidence and stability?

20. What specific actions can you take to develop Christian character?

21. What part does focusing on eternity play in your character development?

22. How can you become more focused on eternity?

23. Memorize 2 Peter 1:10.

Lesson 3

Trusting God's Sure Word

Believers can rely on the trustworthiness of God's Word.

2 Peter 1:15–21

"We have also a more sure word of prophecy; whereunto ye do well that ye take heed, as unto a light that shineth in a dark place, until the day dawn, and the day star arise in your hearts" (2 Peter 1:19).

An emergency room doctor says it's not the trauma he treats in the ER that will kill most of his patients: it's a lifetime of making unhealthy choices that lead to death. So when your doctor tells you to lose weight, watch the cholesterol, exercise—you know the drill—it's wise to heed his advice.

Getting Started

1. How seriously do you take your doctor's orders?

2. What is the weirdest order a doctor has ever given you?

29

3. What part does trust play in determining whether or not people follow a doctor's orders?

In 2 Peter 1:15–21 Peter deals with the need to trust God and His Word. He presents the fulfillment of prophecy as well as his personal testimony concerning Christ's transfiguration as reasons to trust and obey God's Word.

Searching the Scriptures

With his death on the horizon, Peter is determined to continue his work. He is concerned about the next generation of Christians and covets their continued growth in grace and truth. He fears they will let absentmindedness stunt their growth. So he wants to nurture them and prepare them for the time to come.

Peter's Endeavor

The expression "these things" appears four times in 2 Peter 1 (vv. 8, 9, 12, 15). "These things" refers to the truths of godly living, character development, and making salvation certain. It is one thing to know the truth and to be well established in it, which is foundational (v. 12), but it is another thing to have these truths always in the forefront of one's mind.

Peter had these things in the forefront of his mind. In particular, his experience on the Mount of Transfiguration reinforced his expectations about the future (vv. 16–18). It reinforces ours as well. Peter's outlook on his approaching death is a model for us.

4. How would you rate your confidence level in God as you consider your future?

5. What has helped to give you that level of confidence?

Christ's Majesty

Peter wants believers to know that the Bible is trustworthy. We can trust it concerning the "these things" he writes about. He supports his case by affirming the trustworthiness of the prophetic Scriptures. God's Word is true: We can trust it as completely accurate!

6. If prophetic Scripture was only 95 percent accurate, how would that 5 percent of inaccuracy affect your confidence in the rest of Scripture?

In verse 16 Peter affirms the second coming of Jesus Christ through the testimony of the three apostles who witnessed His transfiguration (Matthew 17:1–8).

7. Why might religious scholars want to discredit the doctrine of the Second Coming? What might they be trying to avoid?

Peter, along with James and John, watched as a metamorphosis took place: the inner glory of Christ's deity shone through His body in exactly the same way it will when He returns (16:28).

8. Read Matthew 17:1–8. What impresses you the most about Christ's transfiguration?

Critics reject the teaching of Christ's supernatural entry again into human history because they reject supernaturalism. Peter argues that the revelation of Jesus Christ at His transfiguration was a supernatural event that pointed clearly to His supernatural revelation at His future coming.

What Peter and the others wrote is not to be placed among the popular myths of the day about gods descending to earth (2 Peter 1:16). The prophets foretold Christ's return (v. 19), Christ affirmed it (Matthew 16:28), and the apostles witnessed Christ's revelation of it (2 Peter 1:16).

The Voice of God

The three witnesses to Jesus' transfiguration needed an explanation of what they saw. And God spoke from His excellent glory, honoring His Son (v. 17).

9. Read 2 Peter 1:17. What must we conclude about Christ based on the Father's words about Him?

Peter asserts that he heard God's voice from the "holy mount" (v. 18). This mountain may not have seemed impressive to others, but to Peter, James, and John it was the place where God revealed Himself in glory and by His word. Therefore, it was holy.

Because they were eyewitnesses, the apostles have the right to give the only true interpretation of the historical event (v. 18). The focus is not on the encounter with Jesus, but on what God said. The Bible is not the record of a subjective religious quest of its writers. The apostles were present on the mountain in a real-life experience. They testified later to what they had seen and heard.

The Certainty of Belief

Peter's experience on the Mount of Transfiguration confirmed the Old Testament prophecies of Christ's return. So Peter is convinced more than ever before about the certainty of God's promises. The words "we have also a more sure word of prophecy" (v. 19) could read "we have the word of prophecy made more certain." The prophetic word can never become more trustworthy and dependable than it has been since God spoke it. Therefore, we must pay attention to it!

10. Read 2 Peter 1:19. What should our overall response be to the sureness of God's Word?

With the mountaintop revelation, the Old Testament promises were underlined and given further confirmation in the minds of Peter's readers and our minds as well. Peter writes to strengthen his readers', and our, faith in God's Word (vv. 12, 13).

Peter then exhorts us to continue to pay careful attention to the prophetic message (v. 19). This follows logically his affirmation of the reliability of the Old Testament Scriptures. The Scriptures are like a light shining in a dark place. The "dark place" is the present world. The word "dark" refers to a squalid, dirty place like the filth and gloom of a dungeon. It is descriptive of the present degenerate condition of the whole world, engulfed in moral and spiritual darkness (Ephesians 6:12).

We have the sure word of Scripture to guide us so we need not lose our way doctrinally or morally as long as we live or until Christ returns.

11. What do you think your life would be like without the light of God's Word as you lived in the present spiritually dark world?

Peter describes Christ's return as the dawn of a new day with the appearance of the morning star. The "day star" is Venus, which catches the sun's rays just before the dawn, thus promising daytime. Peter writes that the day star will arise in our hearts. This is the subjective result of Christ's literal return. He will fulfill our heartfelt hope in His return and in the reliability of God's Word. Our whole course of living is to be governed by God's Word, due to its certainty; for it is the truth.

12. If we truly believe in the trustworthiness of God's Word, how should that belief practically affect our lives?

13. Does your life demonstrate that you believe in the trustworthiness of God's Word?

The Origin of Prophecy

In 2 Peter 1:20 Peter asks us to reflect on the origin of Scripture, which is of primary importance. The prophetic Word did not originate of itself, and the reliability of the faith that we believe rests upon its origin.

Several ideas exist to explain Peter's statement that none of the Scripture "is of any private interpretation" (v. 20). First, the meaning of a prophetic text is not a matter of any one person's private interpretation. Second, a text of Scripture cannot be interpreted by itself, for a text must be interpreted in the context of other Scriptures. Third, individuals are incapable of understanding the Scriptures, so the church must interpret the Scriptures for Christians. Fourth, no prophecy has its origin with the prophet himself.

The fourth view provides the best understanding of verse 20. The meaning of the phrase "any private interpretation" can be paraphrased to read "no individual released" the Scriptures. The meaning is that none of the writers of Scripture unleashed the text. Peter explains that the prophets did not originate Scripture as an act of their own wills (v. 21). Each prophecy originated in God's will, not in the will of any writer. Verse 21 is a key text on how the Scriptures were produced. Peter is therefore addressing the origination of Scripture, not its interpretation.

14. Why is establishing that Scriptures came from God so important?

15. How might you treat the Scriptures if they were the result of man's will instead of God's will?

The writing of the Scriptures involved dual authorship (v. 21). "Holy men of God spake" indicates this fact. They were moved along by God's Spirit as they wrote. The word "moved" is used in Acts 27:15 and 17 of a ship caught up and driven by the wind. Men wrote, but God superintended the process so that what they wrote was His Word.

God spoke to men; then they spoke (2 Peter 1:21). He spoke the exact message they were to communicate. God did not give them the basic ideas that He wanted "inscripturated" and then let them phrase His thoughts as they wished. On the other hand, God did not dictate His Word to the human writers as if they were stenographers.

Peter presents the balance between human authorship and God's authorship (v. 21). It was not a matter of equals. The prophets spoke only because God spoke. The Scriptures did not originate with the ingenuity of men, but with God. They did not "release" or "untie" the texts of Scriptures. Scripture is not the result of human imagination or speculation. God spoke to and through the human penmen.

The energizing force in the production of Scripture was the Holy Spirit (v. 21). He carried the writers along, for they were under His control. This "carrying along" resulted in a document that is without even the slightest taint of human error. The Scriptures are inerrant.

16. Why do people try to discredit the inspiration of Scripture? What personal desires are driving their attempts?

The Spirit of God directed the writers of Scripture regarding the very words to write (v. 21). Their individual personalities and styles, however, were not violated. God used their personal backgrounds, life situations, and education. This is why we say that God did not use mechanical dictation in inspiration. The writers were not passive participants, but instead they actively cooperated with the Holy Spirit while writing God's Word. God used men in the production of Scripture even as He uses men to accomplish His purpose in other endeavors.

17. Does inspiration make complete sense to you? What about the process is hard for you to comprehend?

18. Does inspiration need to make complete sense to you in order for it to be true? Explain.

Making It Personal

19. How has the trustworthiness of God's Word helped you in a particularly difficult time in your life?

20. What common issues are present in the lives of believers—including you—that can be brought under the truth of God's trustworthy Word?

21. Identify a personal problem that you can take to God's Word. Choose two verses to memorize that address your problem.

22. How might you be ignoring God's clear Word? Deal with your disobedience by confessing it to God and seeking His enabling to begin to obey His Word.

23. Memorize 2 Peter 1:19.

Lesson 4

Danger Ahead

Christians need to be on the alert for the appearance of false teachers among them.

2 Peter 2:1–9

"But there were false prophets also among the people, even as there shall be false teachers among you, who privily shall bring in damnable heresies, even denying the Lord that bought them, and bring upon themselves swift destruction" (2 Peter 2:1).

C aution: This machine has no brain. Use your own." So read a sign posted on a piece of machinery not meant to be run brainlessly. The sign, though silly, makes a point. The worker running the machine is responsible for his own safety. He can't count on the machine to protect him.

Getting Started

1. How do you respond when you see a danger sign? Do you respect it or disregard it?

2. What is the silliest danger sign you have ever seen?

3. How would you respond if your church had a danger sign on the front door that read "Beware of False Teachers!"? Would you see that sign as silly?

Just as there are teachers of truth in the church, so there will be false teachers too. Peter warns his readers, including us, about false teachers.

Searching the Scriptures

The Appearance of False Teachers

While Israel had a noble succession of true prophets, the nation was plagued often by false prophets. Peter writes that just as there were lying prophets among the people of Israel, there would be false teachers among God's people of his day.

4. Read 2 Peter 2:1. Should we expect false teachers to infiltrate groups of believers today too? Explain.

5. Read Acts 20:29. How did Paul describe false teachers?

6. How does that description help you to understand the seriousness of false teachers?

These false teachers arise from within the church (2 Peter 2:1), but they do not identify themselves with large signs around their necks.

7. What procedures might help a church put in place to identify false teachers who desire to spread their beliefs through the church's teaching ministries?

False teachers are false because they mislead God's people with their lies. They claim to be God's spokesmen while they speak false things that seem plausible to some. Teachers of God's truth held a very high place in the early church. Such is the case today and rightly so.

The Denials of False Teachers

False teachers are smugglers of erroneous doctrines (v. 1). They secretly and deceptively introduce heretical teachings. Their doctrines are destructive, which is the meaning of "damnable." These teachings lead their adherents to the judgment of eternal condemnation.

The doctrines of false teachers are their own heretical opinions (v. 1). Heretical doctrines are opinions that are clearly contrary to Biblical teachings. Such opinions may destroy the confidence that some have in the true faith. After their confidence is shaken, then they become easy prey for religious error.

8. Why would false teachers go so far with their false teachings as to deny Jesus (v. 1)?

At the heart of their heretical teaching is the denial of the redemptive work of Jesus Christ. In their denial they deliberately refuse to accept the truth reveled in the Scriptures about the person and work of Jesus Christ. They are misguided, but more than that they refuse God's truth in preference to their own views on salvation. They profess to be something they are not. They carry their Bibles and use orthodox terms, but with unorthodox meanings. Their views are reinterpretations, which amount to misinterpretations of sound doctrine.

9. Why should we be wary of a teacher who uses the words "new perspective" to describe his teachings about a particular fundamental of the faith?

The Destruction of False Teachers

The outcome of their denial is sudden destruction, which will come upon them abruptly. The idea of the word "destruction" is not annihilation, but everlasting ruin (3:16). This ultimate destiny of false teachers indicates that they were never born again. A saved person can never lose his salvation and will follow Christ (John 10:28, 29).

Peter proves his point by exposing the false teachers' creed and their conduct in the remainder of this letter. They deliberately flout the rule of Christ by seeing how far they can go. These are not Christ's disciples.

A Successful Following

10. Why might someone follow such a false teacher?

The false teachers become popular with many followers, who embrace their heretical opinions. Their doctrines of denial are infectious, and their converts adopt the false teachers' shameful manner of life (2 Peter 2:2). Peter describes this lifestyle as "pernicious," which means unbridled lust. This is why Peter condemns the false teachers so vehemently. They follow morally unrestrained conducts of behavior in the name of Christianity.

11. Read 2 Peter 2:2. Why are false teachers often known for being driven by sinful lusts?

Teachers and their disciples will bring their sexual immorality into the church (v. 2). Their doctrine and corresponding lifestyle are not on the side of God's truth, but against it. This will cause many who observe their lifestyles to blaspheme the way of truth. The "way of truth" is sound doctrine and its corresponding godly lifestyle. Such blasphemy will have a disastrous effect on the church. The way of error, not the way of truth, is to blame for the immoral conduct of these people. The warning that ungodly conduct brings reproach on God's name is clearly illustrated here.

Merchandising People

Peter reveals the false teachers' inner motive of greed. The ministry for them is a lucrative profession. They increase their income through building up a large following.

12. Read 2 Peter 2:3. How do false teachers treat their followers? Do they care about them?

False teachers commercialize religion by exploiting people with "feigned words," meaning "phony arguments" (v. 3). Peter's stringent denouncement of false teachers expresses God's condemnation over the way in which they flout both the truth and godly living.

13. How might followers of a false teacher respond if they realized that their teacher has been using them to gain their money and support?

14. Do think they would turn to God or away from Him? Explain.

The heretics' popularity and gain will come to a predetermined end (v. 3). These are doomed men on the edge of punishment, for the execution pronounced in the distant past has not been overlooked, neither is it sleeping. God has allowed the delay while He exercises His mercy.

To underscore the certainty of the execution of God's judgment, Peter uses three examples of divine judgment from the book of Genesis. He demonstrates that God has judged in the past and therefore can be expected to judge in the future.

The Fallen Angels

The first of the three examples is the judgment of the angels who sinned, although the text does not mention the specific sin. These angels are confined to Hell (v. 4). The word translated "hell" is "Tartarus," which is the lowest part of Hell. They are incarcerated there in "gloomy dungeons," which is a better translation of "chains of darkness." These fallen angels are being held in the densest darkness, which is the farthest extreme from the dazzling light that they once enjoyed in God's presence. They await the final judgment.

15. What point might Peter be making by listing God's judgment on angels?

The Old World

The second example is the judgment of the Flood (v. 5). The universal Flood of Noah's day is an illustration of God's direct intervention in punishing sin.

Man's wickedness at the time of the Flood was very great, for "every imagination of the thoughts of his heart was evil" (Genesis 6:5). The human race was corrupt to its very core and filled with violence (vv. 11–13). God did not spare the world, but instead brought a flood that destroyed man. In His grace God did spare Noah, his wife, his three sons, and their wives (Genesis 6:10, 18).

Noah was "a preacher of righteousness" (2 Peter 2:5). This description probably refers to his preaching activity not recorded in the Old Testament and to his lifestyle. The building of the ark evidenced his belief in the promise of God's judgment upon the world and His mercy to him (Genesis 6:13, 14). Noah was a righteous, mature man who walked with God (v. 9) and who was, no doubt, mocked by his contemporaries.

Believers live among ungodly people who often mock their faith in God. Noah's perseverance is an example for us to emulate.

16. What does the example of the universal Flood help you understand about God's judgment?

Sodom and Gomorrah

The third example of God's unsparing judgment is His destruction of Sodom and Gomorrah. These two cities were located on the southern shore of the Dead Sea, an area rich in sulfur, salt, and bitumen. God rained down fire and brimstone (Gen. 19:24). The cities were reduced to ashes as an example to future generations of God's hatred of their sins (2 Peter 2:6).

Sodom and Gomorrah were cesspools of sexual perversion (Genesis 18:20). "Sodomy" is another name for homosexuality, which Romans 1:26–28 describes and condemns. God made an example of the cities, thus underscoring the truth that His judgment will eventually arrive on the ungodly (2 Peter 2:6). God's total destruction of these cities brings home to all succeeding generations that ungodliness will end only in ruin.

17. Read 2 Peter 2:6 and Genesis 19:24, 25. How many people of the cities of Sodom and Gomorrah, not including Lot's family, survived God's judgment?

18. What does that answer tell you about the certainty of God's judgment?

In the midst of His judgment upon the cities of the plain, God delivered Lot (2 Peter 2:7). That Lot was a righteous man may come as a surprise after reading the Genesis account. He appears as a man who had strayed a long way from God. While he was a hospitable man (Genesis 19:1, 2), he was also weak (vv. 8, 9), was a drunkard, and was morally depraved (vv. 33–38). He was so deeply embedded in Sodom that he had to be dragged out (v. 16).

Peter tells us that Lot was a righteous man who was distressed terribly by the intemperate behavior of the wicked citizenry of Sodom (2 Peter 2:7). His rescue was due entirely to God's grace. God shows His grace to humans because of Who He is, and not because of who humans are.

Lot's soul was distressed daily (v. 8). The conduct of his neighbors was torture to his inner being, which is an evidence of his righteousness. Yet he continued to live in Sodom until the Lord removed him forcibly.

Like Lot, believers should be distressed by what they see and hear. Lot lived in a world like ours, facing pressures to conform and compromise. Unlike Lot, believers must be concerned that their moral sensibilities stay sharp so they don't begin to tolerate pagan values and lifestyles.

God knows how to deliver the godly out of trials (v. 9). He also reserves the ungodly for punishment at the future day of judgment.

19. Read 2 Peter 2:9. Have you ever been tempted to think that God has forgotten how to judge the ungodly? If so, what were the circumstances?

Lot had to endure years of internal distress for his decision to live in Sodom. Yet God delivered him in His own time. While both deliverance and judgment may seem to be delayed, they will come according to God's timetable. In the meantime the ungodly are being reserved for the judgment to come.

Making It Personal

20. How much of your life is controlled by your flesh?

21. Do you need to confess any tolerance for sin in your life?

22. How can you strengthen your understanding of God's truth?

23. What opportunities to strengthen your understanding of God's truth should you take advantage of in your church?

24. Memorize 2 Peter 2:1.

The Way of Balaam

The false teachers who will arise in the fellowship of believers will be morally degenerate in character and conduct.

2 Peter 2:10–16

"Which have forsaken the right way, and are gone astray, following the way of Balaam the son of Bosor, who loved the wages of unrighteousness" (2 Peter 2:15).

Some people have trained their pets to speak simple phrases or even sing a song. A parrot was actually known to announce "I'm bored" when he felt neglected. But no pets, including the bored parrot, can carry on an actual intelligent conversation. For some people, the fact that their pets can't speak is a really good thing! Oh the tales they could tell!

Getting Started

1. If your pet could speak, what do you think it would say to you?

2. How would you react if your pet's message to you included words of rebuke?

Today's lesson includes words of rebuke from an animal that had good reason to speak up. The account helps us to see the importance of considering our motivations for serving God.

Searching the Scriptures

Fleshly Indulgence

Peter characterizes false teachers as those who continually indulge the flesh, the sin nature that all of us possess. Believers also possess a new nature in the Holy Spirit, which is engaged in a warfare with our fleshly desires. This is the conflict that Paul describes. The false teachers know nothing of this conflict, for they have only one nature that controls them (2 Peter 2:10). This is the reason they long only for that which is depraved.

3. What are some examples of false teachings that would appeal to the flesh?

False teachers also despise authority (v. 10). This despising of authority is understandable, since they are given over entirely to serving their own interests. They set their goals to gain whatever they want. They even perform good deeds because the deeds fit their carnal desires in some way. Matthew 6:24 tells us that no person can serve two masters. When self is the master, all other authority is disdained.

4. What have you noticed about your flesh's relationship to authorities in your life?

5. Which authorities does your flesh dislike submitting to the most?

From verse 1 of this second chapter, it is obvious that the false teachers despise Jesus Christ as the Lord. Their repudiation of authority includes local church leadership and all other authorities.

Peter describes them further as presumptuous and self-willed (2 Peter 2:10). They are bold and given only to the things that matter to them. The brashness of the false teachers is seen in their slander of church leaders, or "dignities." These false teachers are insubordinate to the leadership, who have the responsibility to rebuke them for their heretical doctrines and perverse lifestyles. In turn, the apostates blaspheme without hesitation.

6. Philippians 2:3 and 4. How do false teachers line up with Paul's instructions in these verses?

Beyond Angels

The angels, although stronger and more powerful than humans, nevertheless refrain from indicting other authorities. By contrast, the false teachers have gone beyond the angels in their self-assertion and disparagement of authority (2 Peter 2:10). They are without the restraint that the angels exercise by not bringing even righteous indictments.

Peter does not identify a specific occasion when angels refused to bring a condemnation against an authority (v. 11). However, he is probably referring to the dispute that the archangel Michael had with the Devil over the body of Moses, about which Jude writes (Jude 8–10). While Peter makes no direct reference to the story, he could expect that the first readers of this letter knew it; for this story was well known at the time. The story is that Michael refused to seize the divine prerogative, but left it with the Lord to administer the rebuke of Satan. Satan had no right to Moses' body, and Michael contended with him for that reason. However, it was the Lord Who had the right and responsibility to reprimand the Devil.

Irrational Behavior

7. Why might you describe a person as a brute beast?

Peter launches into a direct attack on the false teachers. These men behave like irrational animals, for they adapt themselves to the sensual desires of the body. They are irrational in behavior, therefore, because they follow their passions while neglecting rationality. They leave God out of their thinking and seek to serve their own lusts (Romans 1:28–31).

Peter points out that wild animals are born to be captured and slaughtered (2 Peter 2:12). Therefore, he extends no ministerial courtesy to these apostates. In verse 3 he refers to the divine retribution that neither lingers nor sleeps. The apostle has delineated clearly that eternal judgment will not be averted for these promoters of pernicious doctrines.

Sensuality is self-destructive (v. 12). In the end the person who is controlled by his fleshly appetites loses all. Most tragic of all, he loses his never-dying soul to an eternal existence in Hell (Matthew 13:41, 42).

Peter's unmasking of these men is devastating to their persona and arrogant claims as religious teachers. The apostle exposes them as irrational people who pour out abuse on things about which they are ignorant. While posing as religious authorities, they demonstrate their own spiritual bankruptcy (2 Peter 2:12). They blaspheme the things of God's truth, which they do not really understand. They are ignorant even of their own lack of moral restraint and its consequences.

8. Do you think Peter is being overly harsh in his treatment of the false teachers? Explain.

Spots and Blemishes

9. Read 2 Peter 2:13. How might false teachers be like stains and blemishes on church fellowship?

The ultimate judgment to fall on these false teachers is righteous. God renders judgment to every person according to his or her own deeds (Romans 2:6). God could not be righteous otherwise. While individuals forget their accountability to God and His principles of judgment, He does not.

Peter points out to us that these men are so shameless and abandoned to sin that they engage in their sinful addictions in the light of day (2 Peter 2:13). Normally people wait for the cover of darkness to carouse, because of the shame involved. Apostates, however, involve themselves in daylight debauchery. Their godliness is only outward and is obviously a hollow shell.

Peter writes that the false teachers will feast with the church (v. 13). He refers specifically to the fellowship meals of the church. These are the family gatherings of Christians, or social events, which would include the Lord's Supper. The false teachers taint the fellowship by their continual depraved behavior. The fellowship meals are disfigured, as it were, by their conduct. The meals become occasions for them to sensually satisfy their physical cravings.

The character of these false teachers is the very opposite of Christ's character, which was without any moral spot or blemish (1 Peter 1:19). They also fall short of the moral character God prescribes for His church (Ephesians 5:27). Their presence is a horrendous blight on the fellowship of God's people.

10. Why would letting a false teacher stay in a church actually be the unkind action to take toward the false teacher?

Cursed Children

While they join in the church fellowships, they lust after every woman as if she were a potential adulteress. The phrase "having eyes full of adultery" (2 Peter 2:14) can be translated "having eyes full of an adulteress." It is simply impossible for them to look at any woman without reflecting on the possibility of persuading her to gratify their lusts.

The thirst of these men for sexual sin is never quenched. Lust is always an irritant but is never satisfied. It always leaves a man longing for more and brings him into uncontrollable bondage.

11. Read Romans 6:6, 7. What is the only hope for those who are under the uncontrollable bondage of sin?

False teachers are also actively engaged in luring the unstable (2 Peter 2:14). The word "beguiling" in verse 14 means "to catch with bait." There is no question that these men are recruiters for their devious ways. Those who become hooked are those who are unstable in their faith. The unstable topple because the differences between right and wrong are effaced by false teachings; consequently, the unstable are left without a foundation. For them, right and wrong are not based on absolute truth, because there is no absolute truth in false doctrine.

12. Why do false teachers as well as others living in sin want to recruit followers to their lifestyle?

False teachers train themselves to desire what is forbidden (v.14). The word "exercised" relates to athletic training. They train from their hearts, coveting those things that they really have no right to have.

Peter does not curse them, but he does see the ultimate experience of God's curse upon them. He is descriptive. Apostate teachers live under the curse of God, as do all who fail to trust Christ for deliverance.

Unrighteous Wages

False teachers resemble the prophet Balaam. He loved money and was willing to pursue it even in disobedience to God. Balak, the king of Moab, tried to use Balaam's prophetic gift to rain curses on the Israelites (Numbers 22:2, 4–7, 17), but Balaam was restrained from so doing by the Lord (23:5–8). Balaam told Balak that the Israelites are God's blessed people (24:10–14).

Balaam could not curse God's people, but he did corrupt them to earn his unrighteous wages from Balak (2 Peter 2:15). He proposed to Balak an idolatrous, immoral scheme that led many of Israel to fall. The awful scene of Israel's false worship and debauchery at Baal Peor is indirectly tied to Balaam (Numbers 25:1–3; 31:16). Balaam could not alter God's view of Israel and thereby curse Israel. So he tried to alter Israel's view of God, and many of the Israelites accepted it. He led them down the path of doctrinal and moral compromise that brought God's curse on them. False teachers reject the Biblical way and follow Balaam's way in promoting idolatry and immorality for personal gain.

Iniquity Rebuked

13. Read 1 Peter 2:16 and Numbers 22:26–30. Why was Balaam rebuked by his donkey?

14. Why is Balaam's beating of his donkey ironic? Think about the purpose for Balaam's trip.

As Balaam journeyed to curse the Israelites for money, if he could, the Lord encountered him (Numbers 22:21–35). An angel blocked his path. Balaam did not see the angel, but his donkey did and was frightened (vv. 26, 27). The donkey tried to avoid the angel. Balaam consequently beat the animal but then was rebuked by the animal for his cruelty (vv. 27–30). The Lord had enabled the animal to see the angel and then to speak to his master. The angel had appeared to oppose Balaam's journey (v. 32). Ironically the donkey had more perception than the prophet (2 Peter 2:16).

This miraculous story is no more nonsensical than any other miraculous story recorded in Scripture. It was a historical event in which God revealed the greed and error of Balaam. The heart of the story is that Balaam knew what God instructed him to do, yet for personal gain he was willing to do the opposite. Peter draws the parallel between Balaam and those who follow his example by flying in the face of God. While God does not rebuke false teachers today by dumb animals, He nonetheless rebukes their folly and madness through the text of Scripture.

15. What should be included in a simple message about motivations for serving God?

16. In contrast to the character and behavior of false teachers, who in your church represents, by character and behavior, a true teacher of God's Word?

Making It Personal

17. How would you characterize the type of person a false teacher is most likely to sway away from the truth?

18. Are you stable in your faith? Explain.

19. Evaluate your motives for serving God. Are you serving Him out of love for Him and a desire to see Him glorified?

20. How will you know if you are relying on the Holy Spirit's enabling for serving God?

21. Memorize 2 Peter 2:15.

Lesson 6

Dogs and Sows

A person's conduct is controlled by who he or she is by nature.

2 Peter 2:17–22

"But it is happened unto them according to the true proverb, the dog is turned to his own vomit again; and the sow that was washed to her wallowing in the mire" (2 Peter 2:22).

Peter describes false teachers through picturesque language. One of the images he uses is that of a pig. A pig by nature will wallow in mud and filth from its youngest days no matter how many times its owner washes off all its dirt and grime. Actually, all that wallowing helps a pig develop good bacteria in its gut and stay healthier throughout its life. Peter's point is that false teachers act according to their nature when they roll in the mud pit of sin. There is no silver lining, though, to their wallowing in sin.

Getting Started

1. What are some common actions of pigs?

2. Would you expect a pig to act any differently? Explain.

A church needs to learn that false teachers act according to their nature. This is an important lesson in protecting a church from false teachers.

Spiritual Bankruptcy

The apostle uses two very colorful metaphors to describe the spiritual bankruptcy of the apostates who creep into churches. Peter speaks of their spiritual dryness as springs without water and their spiritual impotence as clouds driven away by a storm (2 Peter 2:17). Such word pictures portray the truth in unforgettable ways.

3. Read 2 Peter 2:17. What thoughts come to your mind when Peter describes false teachers as waterless wells and clouds that promise rain without delivering any?

The creedal pronouncements of the false teachers are unsatisfying like waterless wells. Waterless wells are a tragic disappointment to Eastern travelers, and so are these teachers. People needing spiritual refreshment for their souls find no relief.

4. Read John 4:13, 14 and 7:37, 38. What did Christ promise those who came to Him?

5. Who do you know who found satisfaction in Christ after placing his or her trust in Him?

False teachers give nothing because they have nothing to give (2

Peter 2:17). They are bankrupt spiritually, and their doctrine offers no real hope and assurance of an eternal relationship with God.

False teachers are also like clouds filled with moisture but blown away by the winds of a storm. Such clouds are unstable and transitory. The hopes of the thirsty are dashed. These teachers have no good news to offer, while pretending to be ministers of the gospel.

6. What does it mean to be spiritually "thirsty"?

7. What are some modern examples of false teachers who prey on people's spiritual thirstiness?

The blackest darkness ("mist of darkness") is reserved for these men (v. 17). Peter's description of their eternal perdition is a reference to Hell as the place of separation from God's presence and fellowship. This place is reserved for those who deny God's truth and propagate heresy instead. The falseness of these teachers' claims to provide light becomes clear by the darkness of their own doom.

Verbal Nothingness

The hollowness of their creed is evidenced also in their speech (v. 18). They allure through extremely bloated words in their religious pronouncements. These insignificant words amount actually to nothing. We could liken their words to a blank scroll.

They make claims about what God will do if people will buy into their programs. Those who follow them end up sadly disappointed.

Their goal is to draw in young Christians by their theological jargon. The word "allure" is a fishing term. They use their exaggerated speech in angling for young Christians. Their bait is promises of unrestrained indulgences in lust and passion. This is the meaning of "wantonness." They no doubt maintain that physical and sexual appetites are God-given and should be satisfied.

8. Why might false teachers want to allure others into their way of living? Why do they care if young believers follow them?

Peter's almost two-thousand-year-old description is written as if the apostle is our contemporary. It fits the arguments for unrestrained sensual gratification propagated today. Some today even suggest that the restriction of natural drives can cause only severe personality disturbances. The truth of the matter is that unrestrained sensual indulgence leads only to unsatisfying sexual experiences, perversion, and, worst of all, the judgment of God.

The potential attraction of some relatively new Christians is due to their level of understanding (v. 18). These are new believers who are just escaping the moral corruption of their unsaved lives. They have had a change of heart and need to leave the unrestrained behavior of their old lives behind as new creatures in Christ. The appeal to them is that while they are saved, they still have the right to indulge in unrestrained sensual experiences.

9. What are some of the long-term effects of living with unrestrained sensuality?

Mastered by Sin

What false teachers talk about sounds attractive, but upon closer examination, it becomes evident that there is a gap between what they teach and their private self-indulgence. The freedom these men offer is not true freedom after all, for they themselves are slaves to morally corrupt living. The apostle has encountered storms on the Sea of Galilee and knows the powerlessness of the crews of small boats facing gale winds. These false teachers are equally out of control and powerless to overcome their lusts. The same is true of those who buy into their religious doctrines.

10. Romans 6:16. What does Paul say about slavery?

There is freedom for those who have placed their trust in Jesus Christ (2 Peter 2:19). We have freedom in our relationship with Him. Is a believer free to do as he likes? No, not if it is a matter of being self-willed. Yes, if it means to serve Christ and not to serve sin. We have been set free from slavery to sin to become slaves to righteousness (Romans 6:17, 18). Christ has redeemed us for that purpose.

11. What is freeing about being a slave to righteousness?

Peter reminds us that a person is a slave to whatever has mastered him (2 Peter 2:19). False teachers are like men in chains who offer freedom, as if it were theirs to offer to others imprisoned in chains. The stark reality of the matter is that these teachers are themselves in chains and fellow prisoners along with those whom they allure.

Entangled Again

Peter describes the false teachers as those who for a time escaped from the moral pollution of the world but then reverted to their old paganism. Peter says their last state is worse than the first (v. 20).

What the apostle says about false teachers is true of their followers as well. Peter refers to doctrinally and spiritually unstable people who turn from a morally corrupt lifestyle to a lifestyle that is morally righteous (v. 20). Then at some point they embrace the teachings of these apostate teachers who preach sexual license as morally acceptable for Christians. The resulting moral relapse is worse than their lifestyle prior to their Christian profession.

12. Why might the people who followed the false teachers be worse off morally after embracing the teachings of the false teachers?

The religious reformation that occurs in the conduct of these teachers is due to their knowledge of Jesus Christ (v. 20). Their knowledge of Christ is, however, only head knowledge rather than heart knowledge. Peter uses no terms about them that would indicate they are Christians. Personal faith involves the inner man. We believe with our hearts and then make a confession with our mouths (Romans 10:10). Their profession did not have roots that extended down in faith to their hearts. The evidence of their spiritual bankruptcy points to an absence of genuine faith. This is why the apostle exhorted believers earlier in this letter to conduct a serious self-examination (2 Peter 1:10).

13. Do you know someone who made a false profession of faith?

14. How long did the person live like a Christian before his or her lack of true faith began to show in his or her life?

The false teachers are entangled like a gladiator caught in the net of his opponent or like a hunted animal in the trap of the hunter (2:20). The irony is that they are mastered by their own sin.

These men are worse off because they reject the truth that is the only source of their salvation. They do not forfeit their salvation, since they were never saved. Their brief reformation is terminated due to their outright rejection of Christ's redemptive work (Hebrews 10:29). Their spiritual state of affairs is tragic.

15. How difficult is witnessing to those who have made false professions of faith?

One of the most startling truths to be found in Scripture is in Peter's conclusion about these men (2 Peter 2:21). It would be better for a person who makes a profession of faith in Christ and then turns from it not to have heard the gospel! This pronouncement underlines the seriousness of defection from the truth.

Peter does not spell out how these people are worse off than before (v. 21). It would seem that their hearts would be more hardened against Christ, their minds more cynical to the truth, and their slavery to sin much more intense—all these things because they have rejected the light of truth.

Peter's reference to their knowing the message of the gospel indicates a factual knowledge only (v. 21). Whatever public confession they made is negated due to their eventual rejection of Christ (v. 1). Their knowledge of the gospel is intellectual only and not a matter of faith. To know Christ truly is to be committed to Him with both the mind and the heart in repentance, faith, and obedience. Peter clearly delineates the issue. What we profess to be is demonstrated or disproved by how we conduct our lives ethically and morally.

True Proverb

Peter concludes his devastating denunciation of the false teachers with two final illustrations. These denunciations describe why the false teachers made the choice to reject God's truth.

The Jewish people detested both dogs and pigs. A dog was a scavenger, and a pig was ritually unclean under the Old Testament law.

16. Read 2 Peter 2:22. What thoughts come to your mind when Peter describes false teachers as dogs returning to their vomit and pigs wallowing in the mud?

A true proverb is illustrated by the false teachers' return to the moral corruption of a pagan lifestyle (v. 22). They are like a dog that returns to its own disgusting vomit and like a sow that was washed but goes back to wallowing in the mud. After an initial display of repentance and outward change, these men provide no evidence that an inward change has taken place. This is the final proof that they never were born again. They are still pagan by nature. Animals do not change their natures. So the dog by its nature returns to its vomit; and the sow by its nature, even though bathed, returns to the pigpen. False teachers with their religious profession, along with some outward religious changes, soon revert to their true nature. Individually, each one of them is still the corrupt "old man" controlled by his lust.

Peter explained the dynamics of the new nature earlier in this letter (1:3, 4). The new nature produces a godly life that brings glory to God and prevents believers from returning to the immoral pigpen of paganism.

A person's character and conduct have their source in what that person is by nature (2 Peter 2:22). He or she may put on an outward demeanor that deceives, but not for long. Conduct must eventually revert to type. A person's creed is what he thinks that rationalizes his conduct.

17. Proverbs 23:7. What does this proverb clearly teach?

Making It Personal

18. How can you do to protect your doctrinal position?

19. What could your church do to better protect its doctrinal position?

20. What should your church do to prepare its teachers, who have such a great responsibility for handling God's Word?

21. What measures should your church have in place to monitor what is taught in the church?

22. Memorize 2 Peter 2:22.

Scoffers of the Last Days

Skeptics who deny Christ's return don't understand God's longsuffering.

2 Peter 3:1–9

"The Lord is not slack concerning his promise, as some men count slackness; but is longsuffering to us-ward, not willing that any should perish, but that all should come to repentance" (2 Peter 3:9).

The average person spends between two and three years of his life waiting. A person who commutes through a city might spend a hundred days or more sitting at traffic lights. Imagine having to spend one hundred consecutive days sitting at traffic lights! Perhaps the monotony would drive us to madness. Fortunately our periods of waiting for things like traffic lights, toast, and people are spread out over a lifetime.

Getting Started

1. What might go through a person's mind when waiting for someone whose arrival has seemingly not occurred "on time"?

2. Do you tend to be pessimistic or optimistic in your conclusions about why a person you are waiting for is late?

Peter answered skeptics who denied Christ's return. He gave God's longsuffering as one of the reasons for God's delay. The sureness of Christ's return and God's longsuffering should spur us on to witness to the lost.

Searching the Scriptures

Stirring up the Mind

Ignorance of God's Word often leads to bad decisions by Christians and to their inability to resolve their problems. The same may be said about our forgetting the truth that we know. We need to review and affirm God's truth constantly in our thinking.

The vehemence of Peter's attack on the false teachers in chapter 2 and now in chapter 3 springs from his pastor's heart (2 Peter 3:1). Peter is spiritually strengthening his brothers in Christ, as he does throughout this letter.

Peter's first letter in verse 1 probably refers to First Peter. In both letters the apostle's purpose is to stimulate Christians' thinking. His reference to their "pure minds" indicates that his first readers are not contaminated by the seductive influence of the false teachers. Keeping the mind pure is important, for the mind is used in spiritual discernment. The Christians to whom Peter writes know the truth but need to be reminded of what they have learned, lest they be contaminated in their thinking (3:1). All believers should consistently use their minds to remember God's truth (v. 2).

3. What would you tell a believer who thinks he knows so much about the Bible that he no longer needs to study it?

4. What are some ways believers can remember God's Word?

The false teachers denied Christ's return (v. 4). But both the prophets and the apostles bore testimony to Christ's return. Peter draws together the testimony of both Testaments to help his readers fully understand God's purpose and plan (v. 2).

Scoffers Will Come

Believers must be aware of the presence of scoffers. Peter gives high priority to this need. The arrival of religious scoffers was known to the apostles. Jude warns his readers in a similar fashion (17, 18).

5. Read 2 Peter 3:3. What might be some advantages of being warned of scoffers before they arrive with their destructive message?

These mockers will appear in the last days (2 Peter 3:3), which are actually upon us today. The last days began with the first coming of Christ (Hebrews 1:2). It is yet to be completed after two thousand years.

A characteristic of the time between the two comings of Christ is the opposition of those who are against Christ and His redemptive work (2 Peter 3:3). These are the false teachers described in chapter 2 of 2 Peter.

These mockers of God's truth follow their own evil wants and pleasures. They scoff at religious truths and practices that contradict their own manner of life. For this reason they reject sound doctrine and moral purity by deriding and berating God's Word.

Since the last days are upon us, then the false teachers are present today as well. Peter's epistles provide us with sufficient information so that we can clearly identify them along with their pernicious doctrines.

Questioning the Promise

The false teachers mock the idea of Christ's return while they live self-indulgent lives. Their intellectual arrogance and sensuality make them opposed to the notion of judgment that is inherent in the return of Jesus Christ (Isaiah 2:1–4).

6. Why might the self-indulgent not want to believe in Christ's return?

The skeptics argue that the promise of Christ's return is unreliable (2 Peter 3:4). Where is the fulfillment of His promised return, they ask? Why has He not returned by now? These critics pose the question and then give a reason for their question. The apostle first responds to their underlying reason and then answers the question. Peter points out their deliberate ignorance and then affirms that Christ will return.

7. How should the imminence of Christ's return affect a believer's life?

The scoffers argue that the universe in which we live is governed by natural law (2 Peter 3:4). All the laws of nature operate today as they have since the beginning, they say. They believe the uniformity of natural law cannot be violated; therefore, a miracle could never occur. To say that Christ will return in power and glory to bring judgment would be a miracle, so they deny His return.

Underlying the skeptic's denial of Christ's return is the denial of the existence of a sovereign God Who created and rules over the universe (v. 4). The skeptics are religious, however, for they worship the creation instead of the Creator (Romans 1:21–23).

8. Which belief takes more faith: God created and sustains the world or the world happened by chance?

Willful Ignorance

The skeptics deliberately choose to be ignorant of and to reject this truth: that God relates to the world He created. Peter provides several examples of their ignorance. His response to the critics' illiteracy is not only the Biblical answer to skepticism, but it is also meant to refresh the minds of believers (2 Peter 3:1, 2).

Peter begins at the beginning, the creation (v. 5). He describes the earth after the dry land appeared on the third day of the creation week

(Genesis 1:9, 10). Peter argues that this creative act was by God's authoritative command. He refers, no doubt, to one of God's creative acts as an example of all of God's creative activity. God called into existence all the things of this physical universe, along with all the laws of nature. The laws of nature therefore cannot explain how things came into existence. The beginning of all things is due to God's work and not to the operation of natural law. God relates to the world as the Creator.

Peter's second example of the scoffer's ignorance is the Flood (2 Peter 3:6). Peter describes the inundation of the earth by the universal flood waters of Noah's day (Genesis 7:11–24). The world of men was deluged. While the Flood was a divine judgment on men (6:5–7), it also interrupted the orderliness and continuity of nature in the pre-Flood world. The world of human beings, with the exception of eight people, perished in the worldwide flood. Peter argues that God has intervened into the world by judgment and disrupted the laws of nature while so doing (2 Peter 3:6). He will do so again when Christ returns. God relates to the world as its Judge.

9. How might today's emphasis on protecting and preserving the environment relate to people's denial of God as the Creator?

Peter's third example of the skeptics' willful ignorance is the present world. Peter distinguishes between the present world, which is "now" (v. 7), and the pre-Flood world, which is "the world that then was" (v. 6). They are different, but the skeptics from their limited perspective think the world has always been the same.

10. Read Genesis 8:22. Why should no one be surprised by the fact that the natural world has continued without much change since the time of the Flood?

God will maintain the agricultural cycle, climatic variations, annual seasons, and the cycle of day and night in nature until the future day of judgment (2 Peter 3:7). God is in control of the laws of nature, for He created them and will sustain them (Job 37:6–13).

11. Read 2 Peter 3:7. How does the truth of this verse relate to the supposed threat of global warming?

As the Creator and the One Who preserves the created order, God can intervene or set aside the processes of nature whenever it fits His purpose (2 Peter 3:7). He will bring all things to a climax in fulfillment of His purposes in His own time. Peter fixes that time as the day of judgment of ungodly men. God relates to the world as its Sustainer.

While we do not now see God judging the world, this is not a sign of His weakness (v. 7). God is absolutely in control, and He will judge the world by fire in the future (Isaiah 66:15, 16; Matthew 3:11, 12), Peter's fourth example. The focus of the fiery judgment will be on ungodly men. God's judging of ungodly men collides head-on with the scoffers' doctrine of living today to satisfy one's sensual lusts without any accountability of tomorrow. These scoffers bring upon themselves the righteous judgment of God (2 Peter 2:1). Peter's words are a warning to all who follow their ways.

12. How might a believer guard against adopting the following doctrine: Live today to satisfy your lusts without any future accountability?

God's Timelessness

Peter reemphasizes the need for believers to remember what the Scriptures teach so he can prevent them from being brainwashed by the skeptics. The apostle begins by prompting believers to think precisely about what God has said about the future.

We must remember that time is not the same to God as it is to us (2 Peter 3:8). God created time when He created the heavens and the earth. Even though God is above time, time has value to Him. And He gives this valuable gift to man.

13. How should the fact that time is a gift affect a believer's life?

14. What does society see as the most beneficial ways to use time?

15. How does society's view of time make living in today's world challenging for believers?

Peter draws his reference to God's perspective of days and years from (v. 8; Psalm 90:4). God deals with us in our time-space world. His dwelling place throughout all generations is outside time. For this reason, a day might as well be a thousand years and a thousand years as brief as a single day. Peter is not providing us with some kind of a formula. He is simply reminding us that God is not bound by time, as is man. An apparent delay in Christ's return is not dillydallying on God's part.

God's Desire

The Lord is not slow in keeping His promises as some men think. Men simply do not measure time on God's timeline (2 Peter 3:9). God is not slow; rather He is patient ("longsuffering"; Exodus 34:6; Romans 9:22). He is patient because of His desire.

16. Read 2 Peter 3:9. What desire of God explains why He appears to be late in keeping His promise to send His Son back to earth?

17. How should this desire affect a believer's use of time?

God is ready always to show His mercy to all (Romans 11:32). He has no pleasure in the death of the wicked, but waits patiently for them to turn from their wickedness.

While Christ's death is sufficient to save all (John 3:16), only those who believe will be saved (5:24). God's patience awaits those who will respond by faith. Clearly Christ's delay in returning is not the failure of His plan, but rather the condition of its ultimate success.

Since God is patient with men, Christians should use the time to witness to the lost and explain that God is patient with them and desires their salvation. Our task of evangelism and discipleship fits perfectly into God's grand scheme of redemption.

Making It Personal

18. How wisely have you used your time recently?

19. What time wasters do you need replace with more meaningful uses of your time?

20. How will you respond to God's longsuffering toward the wicked?

21. To whom will you purpose to witness in the coming week as God gives you opportunity?

22. Memorize 2 Peter 3:9.

Lesson 8

The Day of the Lord

*Believers must look forward to the Day of the
Lord by living godly lifestyles.*

2 Peter 3:10–18

**"Wherefore, beloved, seeing that ye look for
such things, be diligent that ye may be found
of him in peace, without spot, and blameless"
(2 Peter 3:14).**

Websites that help you plan your future abound. One in particular is called myfuture.com. The name of the site makes it sound like a person can visit it to find out what his future holds. In reality it just gives tools to help a person plan college and career choices.

Believers should plan for the future with careful diligence—not only for future years on earth, but also for endless years in eternity.

Getting Started

1. Is planning for the future a critical part of your job? If so, what might be the consequences of failing to plan?

2. How much thought do you give to the future in your personal life?

We as believers should live in light of the coming Day of the Lord. Doing so will give our lives purpose and value in this life and forever.

Searching the Scriptures

The Day of the Lord is the future period of time in which the events of the tribulation period, Christ's return to the earth followed by His millennial reign, and then the renovation of the universe will occur. Peter's focus on the Day of the Lord is on the disappearance of the present heavens and earth and the appearance of the new heavens and the new earth. This dramatic change will occur following the millennial reign of Christ (Revelation 20:4; 21:1).

Passing Away of the Old

Christ will return for the church with the Day of the Lord beginning shortly after the Rapture (1 Thessalonians 4:13–18; 5:1–4).

3. Read 2 Peter 3:10. What is Peter's description of what the coming of the Day of the Lord will be for those who are unbelievers?

The blatant denial of Christ's return by false teachers contributes to the unbeliever's attitude of unexpectedness (2 Peter 3:4).

Peter describes the threefold effect of the Day of the Lord on the present universe (v. 10). First, the heavens will pass away with a great roar. Second, the elements will melt due to a fervent heat. Peter is not describing a drastic climatic change or global nuclear holocaust, but a blistering devastation of the present universe. This is the passing away of the present heavens and earth at the conclusion of Christ's millennial reign on the earth (v. 10). Third, planet Earth and all that is a part of it will be consumed by fire. The present order of things is only temporary, for everything material has the stamp of oblivion on it. Those who hold on to the earth and the things of this earth as though permanent are in for a big surprise.

4. How might you use 2 Peter 3:10 as a witnessing tool in a conversation about global warming?

Peter makes the impending disintegration of the universe the impetus for a personal challenge to us (v. 11). He pointedly asks us: "What kind of people should we be?" In the light of these events, we should be living lives of holiness and godliness. We are to live for eternity instead of living for time.

Expecting the New

While looking forward to Christ's return and all the attendant events, we are to be "hasting" its coming (v. 12). The root meaning of "hasting" is "speed." Those who deny Christ's return charge God with the inability to bring the Day of the Lord. This is not the case.

Peter again describes the coming of the fiery disintegration of the universe (v. 12). The expectation and desire of God's people has a broader scope than just entrance into Heaven. Peter describes believers as those who earnestly expect the ultimate rearrangement of the universe. To desire God's will is to desire what God will do for His glory.

The rearrangement of the universe results in the appearance of new heavens and a new earth (v. 13). God will not abandon His creation, but instead He will renew it in accordance with His promise.

5. Read Isaiah 65:17. What will happen to our memories of our current earth?

6. Read Isaiah 66:22. What does God say will be true of the new heavens and new earth?

7. How do these facts underscore the silliness of living for today?

Righteousness will characterize the new heavens and the new earth (2 Peter 3:13). God will totally remove evil, and all who live in the new order of things will be righteous (Matthew 13:41–43).

The ultimate destiny of humankind awaits Christ's return and the judgments, transformation, and the blessings that come with it (2 Peter 3:13). The new heavens and the new earth will be part of the blessings designed for us. Included in the new heavens and the new earth is the heavenly city, which comes down out of Heaven (Revelation 21:2–5). There the saints of God, the angels, and the triune God will dwell (Hebrews 12:22–24).

8. Revelation 21:2–5. What about Heaven motivates you to serve God?

The unsaved will have no access to the heavenly city (Revelation 21:1), for they will be kept forever in the Lake of Fire (20:15). False teachers scoff at the divine revelation detailing the future destiny of unbelievers. The idea of an eternal judgment rubs against the grain of their spiritually darkened conscience.

Moral Purity

9. How often do you think about eternity?

10. What helps you to focus on eternal matters?

The future renewal of the universe involves each of us. We should each look for these things to take place and should each be preparing for them. Peter exhorts us to give intense efforts to being morally pure (2 Peter 3:14). This is another exhortation to make our calling and election to salvation certain in our own minds and hearts (2 Peter 1:10). When we are confident in our relationship with the Lord, we have peace with Him (3:14).

The pattern for our lives is Jesus Christ, Who is without any moral blemishes or spots (1 Peter 1:19). Peter uses spots and blemishes to describe the false teachers (2 Peter 2:14). We must distance ourselves from their doctrines and lifestyles.

Recognize God's Long-suffering

Peter turns again to the question of the perceived delay in Christ's return. The delay need not bring any disillusionment to God's people. It is logical to those who deny the lordship of Jesus Christ (2:1) to also deny His return. Peter explains the delay as due to God's patience (3:9). Therefore divine patience is not slackness, but it is salvation (v. 15). This current age is the period in which God is graciously, patiently offering His salvation to the lost. Believers must recognize this fact.

11. What relationship does moral purity in the believer have with God's long-suffering toward unbelievers needing salvation?

The greatest need that human beings have is to be saved, which places the highest priority on the ministry of evangelism (v. 15). This need takes a higher priority than people's physical needs. This priority does not mean, however, that we forgo extending help to those who hunger and who have physical needs. To turn a deaf ear to the needy in the time of their extremities is to fail to demonstrate God's love (1 John 3:17).

12. Why does meeting a person's physical needs often open a door to minister to his spiritual needs?

13. When has a kind deed given you an opportunity to share Christ?

In 2 Peter 3:15, Peter refers to a letter that Paul wrote to the same people who are receiving this letter from Peter. Paul wrote to these Christians to remind them to live in the light of Christ's return. The two apostles are in agreement in the messages they preach.

Paul wrote with the wisdom that God gave him, though he wrote some things that are difficult to understand (v. 16), about subjects such as the triune Godhead, predestination, election, and sanctification. God's Word can be understood, but its study requires our effort in dependence upon the guidance of the Holy Spirit (1 Corinthians 2:13, 14). The study of God's Word requires diligence and careful attention to the words of the text so that we will correctly interpret it (2 Timothy 3:15).

There is a world of difference between distorting the Scriptures and misunderstanding them. The skeptics twist Paul's writings, as well as the rest of Scriptures, out of shape in a deliberate attempt to make the Biblical text say something other than what it means. The Bible is not God's voice if it says only what men want it to say. Peter affirms that Paul's writings are Scripture.

14. Read 2 Peter 3:16. How does Peter describe those who twist the meaning of Scripture?

These skeptics are willfully ignorant of the truth (v. 5), and they are unstable due to the absence of spiritual life (2:17). They twist the Scriptures to fit their own religious views and moral behavior (3:16).

15. How focused are false teachers on eternal matters?

16. Review 2 Peter 2:1–3. What will the false teachers experience as a result of their focus on the present with no regard for eternal matters?

The church is challenged today by the distortion of Scripture in heretical doctrines propagated by religious leaders of all kind. The false teachers' distortion of the Scriptures is a rejection of God's ways and the substitution of their own ways. This irresponsible conduct will bring upon these religious leaders the retributive judgment of God. They will receive precisely what they deserve.

Error of the Wicked

Peter warns us to be prepared for an assault on the truth of God. We must first be sure that we know the truth. Then we must remember God's truth so that we will be able to recognize the erroneous doctrine of the wicked. Peter sees clearly the damage that comes from embracing doctrinal error. He is now on record as having warned us about this damage.

17. What steps are you taking to learn the truth better?

Peter's appeal to be on guard is an affectionate one to us (v. 17). We are "beloved." False teachers may seem so amiable and their teachings so reasonable that the spiritual harm is unapparent. The unwary who know but do not remember God's truth will stumble into serious difficulty.

Believers face the danger of being carried away from their steadfastness of mind (v. 17). Peter's earnest exhortation does not bring any disrepute on the permanence of the salvation of true believers. Failing to heed the warning would result in their being carried away by the doctrine of the false teachers. They would end up useless as servants of the Lord.

18. Why should a believer never relax his guard against false teachers?

Grow in Grace and Knowledge

Peter exhorts us to grow in God's grace and in the knowledge of Jesus Christ. The more we know about Christ, the more we will live in continual dependence upon His grace. This calls for a deliberate and constant effort to bring Christ to the forefront of our thinking. As we maintain this healthy relationship, we grow spiritually. We develop and mature in our Christian thinking and behavior and are able to withstand the challenges of untruth.

19. The word for "grow" conveys the need for consistent growth. Why must we be growing consistently? Can't we reach a level of maturity that no longer demands intentional spiritual growth?

Peter ends his letter by praising Christ as God is praised (v. 18). He is God (1:1) and receives the glory that He shares with the Father (vv. 16, 17).

Making It Personal

20. Have you been growing in your knowledge of the truth?

21. What steps have you taken, or do you need to take, to ensure growth in your knowledge of the truth?

22. How have you become more like Christ recently?

23. In what areas of your life do you need to depend on God for development of Christlike character?

24. Memorize 2 Peter 3:14.

CREATION MOMENTS

Proclaiming Evidence for Truth

THIS WEEK'S CREATION MOMENT

Scientist Fired for Dinosaur Discovery

We are of God: he that knoweth God heareth us; he that is not of God heareth not us. Hereby know we the spirit of truth, and the spirit of error. – 1 John 4:6

If there is an unwritten law in the field of science, it is this: Thou shalt not discover anything that even suggests that evolution could be wrong. And a second unwritten law is like unto it: If you *do* discover anything that undermines evolution, keep it to yourself.

A scientist was fired from his job at California State University, Northridge, after discovering fossil evidence that supports a young earth and then publishing his findings. While at a dig at Hell Creek formation in Montana, scientist Mark Armitage came upon the largest triceratops horn ever unearthed at the site. When he examined the horn under a high-powered microscope, he was shocked to see soft tissue. This discovery stunned other scientists because it indicated that dinosaurs roamed the earth only thousands of years ago rather than 60 million years ago.

In Armitage's wrongful termination and religious discrimination lawsuit, court documents revealed that a university official challenged his motives by shouting at him, "We are not going to tolerate your religion in this department!" Armitage joins a growing number of scientists and educators who have lost their jobs for challenging the sacred cow of evolution. Many institutions of higher learning are no longer interested in pursuing the evidence wherever it may lead. They only care about evidence that leads them straight to their foregone conclusion that evolution is a fact. Creationists, however, need not fear any new scientific discovery because nothing can successfully contradict the Word of God!

Ref: http://www.pacificjustice.org/press-releases/university-silences-scientist-after-dinosaur-discovery. Photo: Mark H. Armitage.

© 2016, Creation Moments. Churches and parents may freely copy these bulletin inserts.

CREATION MOMENTS, INC.

P. O. Box 839 • Foley, MN 56329 • 800-422-4253
If these bulletin inserts are a blessing to you, please consider making a donation of any amount so we can continue to provide this free resource: www.creationmoments.com/donate.

Lesson 9

Truth and Love in the Christian Life

A believer's walk in truth and love includes refusing to accept or support false teachers.

2 John

"Look to yourselves, that we lose not those things which we have wrought, but that we receive a full reward" (2 John 8).

After John Wilkes Booth shot Abraham Lincoln he sneaked his way into the southern state of Virginia on a broken leg and the hope that the southerners would receive him as a hero. His hopes fell well short of his expectations though. His last stop in Virginia was at a farm owned by the Garrett family. While he initially enjoyed the Garrett's hospitality and even stayed in their home, they relegated him to a locked barn when they learned of his crime. The law caught up with Booth while he was locked in the Garrett's barn. The lack of the southern hospitality Booth was counting on led to his demise. The Garrett family learned the hard way that extending hospitality without asking questions can get a person in trouble.

Getting Started

1. What might be some circumstances in which you would withhold hospitality from someone?

2. What might be some circumstances in which a church would refuse to support or fellowship with someone?

This study of 2 John will help you understand walking in truth and
love in relationship to showing hospitality to false teachers.

Searching the Scriptures

During the time of the New Testament, travel was facilitated by
the system of roads built by the Romans and the peace maintained by
the Roman legions. The church took advantage of this opportunity by
sending out traveling missionaries to spread the Gospel. False teachers,
however, were traveling about under the guise of Christian teachers. It
became a necessity for the apostle John to write letters of instruction
as to whom a local church should extend a welcome and to whom it
should refuse a reception. He accomplished this goal in the course of
writing Second and Third John.

Addressees

John identifies himself as "the elder." The title refers to a senior of-
ficer in a local church. John assumes authority over the people for he is
an apostle.

"The elect lady" refers to the church, while "her children" refers to
the members of the congregation (2 John 1). The New Testament often
refers to the church as Christ's bride (Ephesians 5:22–33).

The apostle loves this church, and so do all who know the truth (2
John 1). The "truth" in verse 1 is God's truth revealed in the Scriptures.
The truth binds believers together, for we all share in the same truth.
We have a personal knowledge and relationship with Jesus Christ and
God the Father through the truth.

3. How does your relationship with a person change once you re-
alize he or she is a Christian?

4. What are some differences between your relationships with un-believing co-workers or family and your relationships with believers?

John explains further that the truth is more than what we know intellectually, for it indwells and permeates believers (v. 2). God's truth lives in us as a present, permanent indwelling force. Our love for each other as believers is motivated by this truth. Christian love is by no means mere sentimentalism or human compassion.

Truth makes Christian love discriminating. Our love should not blind us to others' conduct or views that contradict the truth. We must never compromise our allegiance to the truth by our love for others. We must be characterized equally by truth and love, for both works in com-plete harmony in God's plan.

5. How is truth attacked today?

Greeting

John wishes that God would grant his readers grace, mercy, and peace in the truth and love in which they live. These blessings stem from both the Father and the Son (v. 3). There is no other source. Grace and mercy are both expressions of God's love. Grace is given to the guilty and undeserving, while mercy is extended to the needy and the helpless. Peace is the restoration of harmony with God. When we are at peace with God, peace with ourselves and others follows.

6. If a believer is having a tough time getting along with another believer, what might be true of his or her relationship with God?

In his introduction, John has prepared the way for exhortation and warning. He is concerned about the inner life of the local fellowship (vv. 4–6) and the doctrinal danger from without (vv. 7–11).

Walking in Truth

There is much in the local fellowship that gives John cause for rejoicing. He delights in the believers' obedience to the truth. They are doing exactly what the Father has commanded Christians to do. John encourages them to continue to walk in the truth, meaning to believe and to obey God's Word.

God the Father has revealed His truth to us for our personal commitment and obedience (v. 4). He has not granted the option to us to disbelieve the truth or to disobey it. God's revelation carries with it the responsibility of our faithful response to it.

7. Why might believers think that obeying God is optional?

The Commandment

The apostle exhorts the church to continue to do what the believers know to do. He wants them to love one another (2 John 5). God the Father commands that we love one another (1 John 4:7), while the Holy Spirit enables us to love each other in obedience to the command (vv. 11–13). Christian love provides a clear test of the truthfulness of our confession of faith. A confession may be feigned, but it is extremely difficult to counterfeit true Christian love.

8. Why is true Christian love hard to feign?

9. What might be some indicators that a person is feigning love?

How can we be commanded to have faith and to love? How can we be commanded to believe what we do not believe and to love whom we do not love? The answer is that Christian faith is an obedient response to God's self-revelation in Jesus Christ. Faith is not just an intuitive act. Likewise, Christian love belongs to the realm of action, not emotion. It is not an uncontrollable passion expressed involuntarily, rather it is unselfish service undertaken by deliberate choice.

10. Read 2 John 6. How does John characterize love?

While God's commandment is that we love one another (v. 5), so love is walking in obedience to His commands (v. 6). There is a reciprocal relation between love and obedience, with each word explained in terms of the other. Our love for each other is a living response to what God has commanded.

11. What would you tell someone who professes to love God but whose life is characterized by blatant disobedience to God?

Loss of Full Reward

12. Read 2 John 7. How does John describe the false teachers?

13. Why would he use such serious descriptions?

John turns from true believers to the threat of false teachers. Many deceivers have gone out into the world, having left the church due to their doctrinal defection (1 John 2:18, 19). The term "deceivers" in 2 John 7 means "one who misleads." These false teachers are bound together by their rejection of the incarnation of the Son of God. They deny that Christ took on a human body or that He only appeared to be human. These critics are unwilling to accept that God's Son identified Himself with humanity. But according to Scripture, Jesus Christ is fully God and fully human (Colossians 2:9; Hebrews 10:5).

The denial made by these false teachers deceives people and opposes Christ (2 John 7). They identify themselves in spirit with the anti-Christ.

14. Read 2 Thessalonians 2:4. What will the revealed antichrist do?

The presence of false teachers raises a warning flag for John (2 John 8). Believers need to be on the alert. The error of unbelief is subtle and alluring. Christians cannot afford to relax their vigilance, for there is a disastrous spiritual effect if they compromise their doctrinal belief. It would mean a loss of a full reward, but not a loss of salvation.

15. How devastating do you think a loss of reward would be to you?

The phrase "full reward" in verse 8 means that failure would not totally deprive a Christian of a reward. The word "reward" refers to the wages of a working man. It is the fullness of reward that is threatened by the subversive teaching of false teachers. God does not forget what believers have done for Him (1 Corinthians 4:5). All of us will receive reward according to our labor for Christ (Revelation 22:12).

John exhorts us to faithfulness and persistence so that we will not lose any of the reward that is ours to receive from God. It will be our privilege in the future to cast our crowns of reward at Christ's feet in Heaven (Revelation 4:9–11). We will give Him the glory for all that He accomplished through us.

16. Evaluate the following statement: A believer never retires from the Christian life.

Defection from Truth

John moves to a second warning, which is far beyond the loss of a full reward. The word "transgresseth" in verse 9 means "to overstep." John is speaking of those who go too far. They break out of the doctrinal limits of the faith by turning aside from the true doctrine of Christ. Instead of affirmation of the truth professed, there is defection from the truth. The result is not a loss of reward, but the demonstration of an absence of a relationship with God. This is descriptive of false teachers and those who wholeheartedly embrace their doctrines and corresponding moral behavior. They do not possess eternal life, for eternal life is to know God, the Father, and Jesus Christ (John 17:3).

John provides the crucial contrast to those who defect (2 John 9). Those who continue in the true doctrine about Jesus Christ have both the Father and the Son. God is with those who persist in the truth. No person can profess truly to have a relationship with the Father without a relationship with the Son at the same time. The Son is both the revelation of the Father (John 1:18) and the way to the Father (14:6). When we receive the Son by faith, only then do we also receive the Father. There are those today who want God without Jesus Christ. This is clearly impossible, for God says so!

Reception of False Teachers

John expects the false teachers to arrive soon with their pernicious propaganda (2 John 10). Their lack of a true doctrine of the person of Christ will pose a dangerous situation to the church. Therefore, the believers are not to show them hospitality as though they are teachers of the truth. To show hospitality to them would mock God, for the false teachers deny the truth concerning Christ. John exhorts the church to neither receive them officially nor send them on their way with God's blessing.

17. What are some ways a church might show hospitality or cooperate with false teachers today?

The word "house" in verse 10 refers primarily to the early local church, which met in houses rather than church buildings. The church is not to receive any false teachers, for that would place a sanction on their devious doctrine. Further, to bid such a perpetrator of error "God-speed" is to desire his success in his devious work (v. 11). All of this is a blatant contradiction to the truth.

The admonition against showing hospitality applies only to those who are committed to actively and aggressively destroying the faith of believers (vv. 10, 11). The issue is the denial of truth, not disagreements in the interpretation of Scripture among believers. John does not say that the church is to hate and retaliate against deceivers, but it is to keep them at a distance.

18. Why is distancing yourself from deceivers a loving act toward them?

Visiting Soon

John desires to visit them soon because he knows his tone and the expression on his face will help to convey the meaning of his words (v. 12). At his visit, their conversation will encourage their full joy because together they share in the salvation that God provides graciously through His Son. Their discussions will produce more understanding of the truth and the fullness of the joy of knowing God.

Making It Personal

19. What might a commitment to God's Word look like practically?

20. What could you do to strengthen your commitment to God's Word?

21. Memorize 2 John 8.

Lesson 10

Contrasting Leaders

Godly leaders are characterized by love and selflessness.

3 John

"Beloved, follow not that which is evil, but that which is good. He that doeth good is of God: but he that doeth evil hath not seen God" (3 John 11).

Jean-Claude "Baby Doc" Duvalier, former and reluctant ruler of Haiti, treated Haiti's national treasury as a personal bank account while he let his father's old cronies do the actual governing. After ten years in office, he married Michele Bennett Pasquet. Their wedding cost $3 million—a price that angered the Haitian people. The couple ignored the outrage and continued to live to better themselves. Their money came from the drug trade and the sale of Haitian cadavers to medical schools overseas. Eventually Duvalier was exiled. When he returned he was arrested for the embezzlement he habitually engaged in while in power. Duvalier left no doubt in the world's mind that he was a bad leader.

Getting Started

1. Who would you consider to be the best example of a good leader (not including Christ)? Why?

2. Whom would you consider to be the worst bad leader? Why?

John talked a lot about good leaders and bad leaders in his third epistle. We can learn about the type of leader God wants us to be from reading John's short letter.

Hospitality of Gaius

Third John is a letter from John to Gaius to encourage him to show hospitality to Demetrius and to other traveling missionaries sent out by John. This encouragement is needed because Diotrephes is dominating Gaius' church, and he refuses to extend a welcome to the traveling preachers. He also excommunicates any in the church who do.

Both 2 John and 3 John focus on the treatment to be given by the local church to itinerant teachers. In 2 John, the apostle warns the church not to extend hospitality to false teachers. In 3 John, he emphasizes providing assistance to fellow-believers who are sent out as traveling missionaries.

Third John is both a personal and an authoritative letter (3 John 1). John's deep friendship and warm affection permeate the letter. Three times he addresses Gaius as "beloved" (vv. 2, 5, 11). Third John is also an official letter from an apostle. While written to Gaius, the content is to be shared with the rest of the congregation.

Gaius is an influential person in the church. That John writes to him as he does indicates that Gaius occupies a position of responsibility and leadership in that local church. John would not write a letter so outspoken about Diotrephes to anyone but a church leader. The apostle loves Gaius in the truth, which is a genuine love in accord with God's truth.

3. In what sense is John's letter an evidence of the presence of God's love in his life? Do you think he would have taken time to write a letter if he didn't actually love God's people?

Walking in the Truth

The apostle wishes that Gaius will experience good physical health. This desire implies that Gaius is in good spiritual health and that John wishes the same for him physically. This wish does not necessarily imply that Gaius is ill. This reference does, however, provide us with a warrant to pray for the temporal needs of fellow-believers.

John receives a positive report about Gaius from some Christians who visit his church (v. 3). These are traveling missionaries who tell John about Gaius' faithfulness in believing and living out the truth. These comments describe his lifestyle, which is in evidence to the visiting Christian brothers. Gaius walks in love (v. 6) as well as in the truth (v. 4). Christians really cannot walk in one without the other.

John cannot receive greater news than that his children are living in the truth (v. 4). This knowledge gives him great joy. His "children" refers those whom he has led to Christ. After leading them to the Lord, he has a responsibility for their spiritual growth, which is why he writes his letters.

4. What would you say gives you your greatest joy?

5. Read 3 John 4. What is the difference between believing the truth and walking in the truth?

To walk in the truth is more than giving mental assent to it. Believers walk in the truth when they apply God's truth to their behavior. Gaius is a model for us, for he integrates the truth into who he is and what he does. There is an exact correspondence between his creed and conduct.

6. What word would you use to describe a person who compartmentalizes his life?

7. Why must a leader in particular not compartmentalize his or her life?

Supporting Missionaries

John commends Gaius for his hospitality to Christian brothers. These men may have come from John to visit Gaius' church (v. 5). Gaius received them as fellow believers even though he did not know them, for they were strangers to him. Hospitality is required of all Christians, even though it is necessary to refuse it at times to false teachers (2 John 10). Gaius exemplifies the hospitality in which everyone in the church should engage. The traveling missionaries carry back a sterling report to the apostle about Gaius's reception of them (3 John 6). His practical ministry to these strangers is true to his profession of faith in Christ.

8. Why is hospitality an important part of being a godly church leader?

These same men probably carry this letter from John to Gaius (v. 6). John exhorts Gaius to again show hospitality to them. He is to make adequate provision for these men while they are there and when they resume their journey. Gaius is to do this after a manner worthy of God and recognize these missionaries as God's servants.

9. Read John 13:20. How did Jesus point out the importance of hospitality?

John gives three reasons why these traveling missionaries should be supported. First, these men have gone out in Jesus' name (3 John 7). These particular teachers have been sent out by the assembly of believers with whom John is associated.

Second, missionaries have no other means of support than God's people (v. 7). It is inappropriate for those who represent the Lord to seek support from those who do not believe in His name.

Third, believers are fellow workers in the ministry of proclaiming God's truth (v. 8). Missionaries and their supporting churches form a ministry partnership.

10. How should churches treat their missionaries—their partners in ministry?

Censure of Diotrephes

11. Read 3 John 9. Based on his actions, whom does Diotrephes love more than anyone else?

John had earlier written a letter to Gaius' church. Diotrephes either suppressed it or destroyed it because he opposed the apostle. John wrote the letter requesting the church to extend hospitality to the traveling missionaries (v. 9). Diotrephes would have none of this, although it appears that Gaius withstood him.

We do not know why Diotrephes opposes John, except for the fact that he loves to have the preeminence in the church. He is therefore a rival to John, and, no doubt, to any others who pose a threat as potential leaders. John's influence in the church is longstanding, and Diotrephes is troubled by it.

Diotrephes is possessed by an inflated ego and a dictatorial manner. He loves himself more than others. He has gained ascendancy over the rest of the leadership in the church as a self-willed, authoritarian individual.

12. How would you expect Diotrephes to act in a church business meeting?

13. How would you expect him to treat a person with a serious need?

Diotrephes resists John's instructions and refuses to welcome the traveling missionaries who have come from John. Diotrephes does not want John to have the place of preeminence. His self-love and greed of power have erupted in his antisocial behavior.

Disciplinary Action

14. Read 3 John 10. What could happen to a church who leaders seek to avoid conflict at all costs?

John declares that if he comes in person, he will deal with Diotrephes. The issue that John faces with Diotrephes is not doctrinal, for the apostle does not mention such. The conflict between the two is Diotrephes's opposition to John's authority. The apostle must deal with Diotrephes's opposition because of the weakening effect it could have on his position in the church and make it easier for false teachers to influence the congregation.

John censures Diotrephes's behavior on three charges stemming from his misuse of authority (v. 10). In the first place, Diotrephes is guilty of malicious gossip about John and the missionaries. Diotrephes does his best to damage these men's reputation. He finds these missionaries guilty by association, for these missionaries are associated with John.

15. How should a church respond to church members who spread malicious charges against their pastor?

Second, Diotrephes denies hospitality to fellow Christians engaged in the ministry (v. 10). He sees their arrival at the church as an intrusion and responds with vicious innuendoes against John and the itinerant preachers.

Finally, Diotrephes expels anyone in the congregation who extends hospitality to the traveling brothers (v. 10). He forces other believers to be inhospitable or, if they refuse, expels them from the church. Diotrephes actions demonstrate that self-love impairs all relationships.

The apostle John has an unpleasant experience awaiting him when he arrives. But his love of the truth makes it necessary for him to act decisively. Inaction on John's part would be hypocritical. Discipline in the church is never pleasant or easy, but it is necessary for the sake of the truth.

16. What excuses might John have given for not dealing with Diotrephes?

Recommendation of Demetrius

John encourages Gaius to continue doing good deeds and not to give in to any pressure to do evil. Gaius is not to imitate Diotrephes' behavior. This is the specific evil against which John warns. Gaius is to imitate the good, which is to receive his fellow-believers.

17. Who in your church is a godly example of loving hospitality?

John sets forth the contrast between the two habitual ways of life (v. 11). Whether a believer entertains or refuses to entertain visiting missionaries—or faces any moral choice—the principles John presents always apply to Christian conduct. The person who continually does that which is good is of God. By contrast, the person who continually does that which is evil has not seen God. He is not "of God," for his evil way is the product of the darkness of his heart (Ephesians 4:17, 18). He is blind toward God, for evil never arises from a true spiritual perception of God. One who has been born of God has come with the inner eye of faith to see God (John 3:3).

Good Report

John commends Demetrius to Gaius as a model for following the good. Demetrius is one of John's supporters and may be a traveling missionary and the bearer of this letter. Gaius is to welcome him.

Demetrius is well spoken of by everyone who knows him, by the truth, and by John (3 John 12). He walks in the truth of the gospel. His manner of life matches his confession of faith (v. 4). The truth therefore speaks well of him.

John could personally attest to Demetrius's character (v. 12). Gaius knows that John's testimony about the man is true. Gaius has no reason to hesitate to show hospitality to Demetrius. If Gaius has to go out on a limb in showing hospitality because of Diotrephes, then he could do so for two reasons: it is the good thing to do, and Demetrius is worthy.

John hopes to see Gaius in person soon, when he will be able to communicate the other things on his heart and mind. John wishes Gaius God's peace and greetings from friends. John's friends are Gaius's friends as well.

John asks Gaius to greet his friends in the church by name (v. 14). Christians form a network of friends that are ready to encourage and support one another always.

Making It Personal

18. In what ways are you a leader?

19. Have you ever considered whether your leadership was rooted in love? What might be some clues that your leadership is rooted in love instead of selfishness?

20. What can church members do to assure godly leadership in the church?

21. Memorize 3 John 11.

Contending for the Faith

Christians must be zealous in contending for and living out the faith.

Jude 1–9

"Beloved, when I gave all diligence to write unto you of the common salvation, it was needful for me to write unto you, and exhort you that ye should earnestly contend for the faith which was once delivered unto the saints" (Jude 3).

Mauritania, one of the nation's poorest countries, is located on the upper west coast of Africa. The nation is 99.84 percent Muslin and .16 percent Christian. Muslims have dominated the nation for over a thousand years, absolutely forbidding the practice of any religion but Islam. Those who are believers in this nation face beatings and even the death penalty when they are arrested for their faith. A female was beaten by her own family and then tied up for seven months when she converted to Christianity. Being a Christian in Mauritania takes resolve and a zealous faith.

Getting Started

1. What would you list as the top three things in your life that would be worth fighting for?

2. Where would you put "the faith" on your list of things worth fighting for?

Jude's letter has called believers down through the ages to contend for the faith. His message is as appropriate for us now as it has ever been. We should take his message seriously and be ready to be zealous for the faith both by defending it and by living it out.

Searching the Scriptures

The Letter Writer

3. Read Jude 1. How did Jude, the half brother of Jesus, introduce himself in his letter?

4. Why do you suppose he didn't draw attention to the fact that he was Jesus' half brother?

Jude is the brother of James, probably the James who was a leader in the Jerusalem church (Acts 15:13) and the writer of a New Testament letter that bears his name (James 1:1). This means that Jude and James were half-brothers to Jesus. Jude did not consider himself worthy to call himself a brother of Jesus but just His servant (Jude 1).

Jude's letter is not written to a specific church. Jude simply describes the recipients in three ways. They are loved by God, kept secure in their position in Jesus Christ, and called of God (v. 1). The knowledge of God's love, keeping power, and call always provides assurance and inner peace for us, including at times when our faith is critically challenged.

Jude's greeting (v. 2) is a typical first-century greeting, a significant fact in the context of the letter. His heart overflows with love and concern while he warns about those who would, if it were possible, destroy the faith. Jude wishes for an abundance of three things for his readers: mercy, peace, and love.

5. Read Jude 2. How would mercy, peace, and love help Jude's readers as they faced opposition?

The Grave Danger

Jude has a sincere desire to write about the theme of salvation when he takes pen and paper in hand. All believers share in the same salvation, which is, therefore, "common" to all of us. However, Jude is compelled to change his subject.

6. Read Jude 3, 4. Why does Jude feel compelled to change his subject?

Jude sees the encroaching apostasy brought on by the adversaries of God who endanger the church. His love for God's truth and his fellow believers moves him to sound a solemn and serious warning.

Jude's new theme concerns the course of action that his readers must take in the light of the grave danger that has arisen from within their ranks (v. 3). Jude exhorts them to contend intently for the faith.

7. What comes to your mind when you hear the phrase "earnestly contend"?

8. How does earnestly contending for the faith differ from being a negative, contentious Christian?

The term "earnestly contend" means "to endeavor with strenuous zeal and agony." Jude's usage of the term is an exhortation to all believers to struggle offensively against the doctrinal error and moral perversions that false teachers propagate. We contend earnestly when we proclaim the truths of God's Word accurately, clearly, and fearlessly.

9. How has the command to "contend for the faith" been practiced by the church in recent times?

10. What has been the outcome of these practices?

"The faith" is the body of truth that the Scriptures teach (v. 3). Paul warned that some would depart from the faith (1 Timothy 4:1). The faith is the truth by which we are saved and by which we live godly lives. God in grace and wisdom has provided through special revelation a distinct body of truth, which we embrace by personal faith.

11. Why is ignorance of the truth among believers as serious a threat as false teachers are?

12. Do you think you could earnestly contend for "the faith" based on your current understanding of it? Explain.

Jude explains further that our faith has been delivered to us once and for all (Jude 3). "Once and for all" is the meaning of the word "once." There is no room to think that God grants additions and extra insights to it through the years of church history. The Christian faith cannot be changed, for its foundational truths are nonnegotiable. It is irrevocably fixed for us.

Jude then gives the reason why he feels the compelling obligation to change his theme (v. 4). Certain men have secretly slipped into the fellowship with a different kind of Christianity. This infiltration poses a serious danger to doctrinal and moral purity in the church. The men are pretenders who impersonate real Christians. Jude therefore has good reason for his intractable stance on the faith.

Jude describes these men as godless (v. 4). This lack of reverence for God is demonstrated by the way in which they change God's grace into a license for unbridled lust and shamelessness. Their idea is that God's grace permits us to sin.

13. When, if ever, have you seen this type of attitude in people who claimed to be believers?

These men also deny the sovereign lordship of Jesus Christ (v. 4). Such denial leads them to play loose and fast with what God commands. This faulty thinking results in their moral error. They seek to satisfy their fleshly desires, whatever they might be. They teach others to do the same, arguing that God's grace allows it.

These men sound convincing. They have wormed their way into the fellowship by stealth. Jude is saying that we cannot take them at face value. What they say and what they mean are really antithetical in the light of God's truth.

The proponents of these errors must be confronted with the affirmation of the truth. A church pure in doctrine in one generation that becomes doctrinally inclusive will become the heretical church of the next generation.

14. What part might a church's Sunday School curriculum play in perpetuating pure doctrine in a church?

15. What should be the major considerations your church takes into account as they select curriculum for the various age groups in the church?

Examples of God's Judgment

Jude calls us with a tone of solemnity to remember Biblical truths. God does not forget His promises, and neither should we. There is no place for toleration of error due to forgetfulness of the truth.

Jude draws upon three Old Testament accounts of divine judgment (vv. 5–7). All three accounts illustrate the truth that rebellion against God never succeeds.

The first example is taken from Israel's history (v. 5). An entire generation of Israelites fell in the wilderness after having been delivered from Egyptian bondage. Israel's exodus from slavery in Egypt is a pictorial illustration of God's salvation of His people. Against this background of deliverance, there was a rabble of Israelites who chose not to believe, despite the promises of God and the demonstration of His redemptive power (Numbers 14:26–30).

The false teachers are like that generation of Israelites who fell in the wilderness due to unbelief. The men who oppose the truth profess to believe in the fundamentals of the faith while they willingly embrace heresy. They are attracted to an immoral lifestyle and to the belief in a god who allows such. Their god is not the God of the Bible; therefore, they are engaging in a form of idolatry.

The second example is that of the fallen angels (Jude 6). The way in which Jude refers to the incident without any explanation indicates his readers know this narrative well. At issue was the fact that the angels rebelled and God punished them for their rebellion.

The third example is that of Sodom and Gomorrah (v. 7). The judgment of the two cities on the plain south of the Dead Sea serves as a dreadful example of God's judgment on those who give themselves over to the lusts of their sinful natures (Genesis 19:24, 25). The men of Sodom and Gomorrah engaged in a form of sexual relations that was unnatural to them, homosexuality. God has clearly declared homosexuality to be unnatural for man (Romans 1:26, 27).

The destruction of the cities of the Dead Sea plain by a horrific fire is an example of the eternal fire of Hell (Jude 7). This judgment awaits all who oppose God. Though it delay, God's judgment will surely come.

16. How would you characterize the three examples of rebellion and judgment that Jude gave: mild, average, severe?

17. What is Jude conveying by using these serious examples of rebellion and judgment?

Linkage with False Teachers

Jude draws the link between the three illustrations of God's judgment and the false teachers. He sees them as dreamers because they are unrealistic in their thinking about God and morality (v. 8). He is speaking figuratively, for these men are captivated in their thoughts with carnal images produced by the lusts of their sinful natures.

Jude draws three parallels beginning with the contamination of their own bodies. They are like the men of Sodom and Gomorrah in the engagement in sexual abuses. One major evidence of the presence of these dreamers within the churches is the loosening of the standards of sexual morality and the corresponding acceptance of behavior once deemed to be unbiblical.

18. How has the acceptance of sexual immorality crept into churches, particularly mainline churches, in recent years?

Second, Jude says that they scoff at authority (v. 8). They reject authority, as the unbelieving Israelites rejected the authority of the Lord in the wilderness. In the context of Jude's statement, these false teachers deny the sovereign lordship of Jesus Christ (v. 4). This rejection leads to despising human authority, both civil power and church leaders. False teachers often argue that Biblical standards need reinterpretation, because they fit a culture that is long past.

Third, Jude writes that they slander celestial beings (v. 8). This description refers to angels, both good and bad. The case of Michael's refusal to contend with the Devil lends support to this idea (v. 9). Their slander of the angels arises from their rejection of anything and anyone affiliated with God and His program. Angels are clearly associated with God and His program. Angels are slandered when actions and characteristics are attributed to them in contradiction to what God says is true of them.

Jude argues that if the archangel was extremely careful in speaking to a dignity, so human beings should be careful to respect authority (v. 9). The archangel Michael was dispatched by God to bury Moses after his death. The Devil disputed his right to do so. Michael was not disrespectful to the Devil, even under such contention. He referred the dispute to the sovereignty of God by saying, "The Lord rebuke thee."

Making It Personal

Sound doctrine is essential to your spiritual growth. You also need to know sound doctrine in order to defend it.

19. How well do you know doctrine?

20. What steps could you take to understand basic doctrines better?

21. Memorize Jude 3.

Lesson 12

Irrational Beasts

Believers need to know why false teachers think and act as they do because false teachers are a threat to believers.

Jude 10–16

"But these speak evil of those things which they know not: but what they know naturally, as brute beasts, in those things they corrupt themselves" (Jude 10).

Stains are irritating and getting them out can be a nightmare. Coffee is a common drink and therefore a common stain. According to realsimple.com, the best way to get a coffee stain out is to stretch the stained material over a bowl and pour boiling water onto the stain from about a foot above the bowl. Follow up this daring stunt by applying an oil solvent to remove any residual milk stains and a glycerin cleaner to get out any sugar stain. The last step is a normal wash cycle.

Getting Started

1. What might someone imply by calling you a stain?

107

2. How would you respond if someone called you a stain?

Jude likens false teachers to stains as well as four other pictures. His descriptions help us to understand false teachers. His descriptions also cause us to consider whether our lives reflect the way false teachers think and act.

Searching the Scriptures

Destitute of Spiritual Perception

Jude continues his description and denunciation of the false teachers who have crept in secretly among believers. He points to their total lack of spiritual understanding, their blaspheming of God, and their animal-like thinking.

3. Read Jude 10. How would you characterize an animal's thinking?

4. What is Jude saying about false teachers by comparing their thinking to the thinking of animals?

The false teachers toss out large portions of the Bible because they simply cannot understand them. Certain doctrines, admonitions, and warnings in the Biblical text are irrational and offensive to them. The problem of their understanding is really with their reception. These false teachers cannot think on the spiritual level of understanding needed to comprehend God's Word.

5. When have you realized the fruitlessness of arguing with a religious unbeliever about spiritual matters?

While these religionists assume to have superior knowledge, they are in fact ignorant of the truth (v. 10). They sit in judgment on God's Word in a fashion similar to the atheist fool who claims that God does not exist.

It is the Holy Spirit Who enables believers to understand God's truth. The unsaved person, by contrast, thinks naturally. His understanding of God is covered with darkness, and he is estranged from God in his spiritually blind condition. Those who propagate error cannot grasp spiritual truth because they think like brute beasts. Their behavior is then directed by their physical senses.

6. What do you remember about how your understanding of spiritual things changed once you trusted in Christ as your Savior?

The brute perceptions of these men lead to their moral and physical corruption (v. 10). Yet they are accountable for their ways and will experience destruction as a result of them (James 1:15).

7. Should we write off false teachers completely? Are they hopelessly lost? Explain.

While we believers have been renewed in our minds through the new birth, we must constantly bring our thoughts into conformity to God's truth (2 Corinthians 10:5).

Counts of Indictment

Jude pronounces "woe" on the false teachers by using three Old Testament examples. The examples show that the false teachers err in three respects due to their inability to understand God's truth (Jude 11).

First, they are given to manufacturing their own religion. Like Cain they devise their own way of worship in disobedience to God's Word (Hebrews 11:4). Cain was so distraught with God's rejection of his substitute worship that he killed his brother in jealously (Genesis 4:4–9). Cain defied God and despised man. The two go hand in hand.

8. Name some currents examples of people who have rejected God and have despised His followers?

Second, they promote false religion for greed (Jude 11). They rush after Balaam's example. Balaam is the prototype of all the greedy false teachers who lead God's people into doctrinal error and immorality for material gain (2 Peter 2:15, 16). He clued the King of Moab as to how he could get Israel involved in idolatry and immorality (Numbers 25:1–5; 31:16). Israel fell into sin and under God's judgment due to Balaam's doctrine. But Balaam came under God's righteous judgment for his sin shortly thereafter (31:8).

9. Why is the fact that false teachers are associated with greed not surprising?

Third, they rebel against God's authority figures (Jude 11). They imitate Korah, who led a full-scale revolt against God's delegated authorities, Moses and Aaron (Numbers 16:1–4).

10. Read Numbers 16:28–33. Who were the sons of Korah ultimately rejecting with their rebellion against Moses and Aaron?

The Lord responded to the rebellion of the sons of Korah with His judgment. Jude announces that false teachers have "perished" likewise. He uses the past tense as if their judgment has already occurred. This is

God's way of denoting the certainty of their ultimate destiny.

Descriptive Pictures

Jude uses five images to describe the hazard that these false religionists are to God's people. First, false teachers are stains on Christian love feasts (Jude 12). The love feasts in the first century are ordinary meals at which Christians pray together. The Lord's Supper usually followed the meal. The false teachers feigned spirituality without fear or hesitation as they participated in the Lord's Supper.

The presence of false teachers poses the danger of polluting the fellowship of God's people. They stain the fellowship through their hypocrisy. They participate outwardly as though one with believers, while denying the Lord in their minds and hearts.

Throughout the love feasts the false teachers are selfish in their behavior (v. 12). Their motive for participating in the love feasts is the personal gain of their own visibility and prestige. They feel no fear of the Lord when they mock the death of God's Son, as observed in the Lord's Supper.

11. Read 1 Corinthians 11:27–29. Why should the false teachers have taken the Lord's Supper more seriously?

Second, apostates are like clouds that promise rain but do not give a drop to the thirsty ground (Jude 12). This vivid example portrays the uselessness of their teaching. While professing to have a great knowledge about God, there is nothing to offer as nourishment for a believer's spiritual life. Then like clouds without rain, they are soon gone, being blown away by the wind. They are spiritually unstable in their own souls.

12. What would you predict concerning the long-term success of a false teacher given the fact they offer no real spiritual help to their followers?

Third, false religionists are like trees that produce no fruit in season (v. 12). Their appearance instead is like fruit trees in late fall, long past the harvest. Their growth has stopped, and their branches are bare when they should be fruitful. They are twice dead, for they have also been uprooted. The thrust of this picture is that they have no spiritual roots and therefore no fruit.

13. Why will those who produce fake fruit to cover for their lack of true spirituality eventually be revealed for who they really are?

Fourth, false teachers are like the wild waves of the sea (v. 13). Wild waves of the sea rage back and forth and produce only filthy scum, which is found littered on the seashore when the tide recedes. These false teachers produce only the froth of their own shameful actions. They are known only for the moral filth of their immoral contamination.

Fifth, religious apostates are like aimless stars that move across the sky (v. 13). The reference is to comets or meteors. These provide no guidance for navigation, as do fixed stars. The description depicts the eternal darkness of the doom reserved for these ungodly men.

14. Given the pictures of false teachers, how should a church respond if one tried to enter its fellowship?

Prophecy of Judgment

Jude refers to a prophecy that supports the inescapable judgment on the apostates that will accompany Christ's return. Prior to the Flood, Enoch predicted this judgment on the ungodly. Jude's reference in verse 14 corresponds to his previous statement that these men were ordained "before of old" to condemnation (v. 4).

15. Read Jude 14, 15. How do you think the false teachers who heard this passage responded to it?

Enoch, or Henoch, is the seventh from Adam. This prophecy of Enoch's is not found in the Old Testament. Jude is quoting from a book supposedly written by Enoch. This book is a part of the Pseudepigrapha, which is a large body of Jewish writings composed between 200 BC and AD 100. This name is attached to these non-canonical works because they are unauthentic. Many of the books in the collection bear the names of famous persons from the Old Testament. These books, however, did not come from their pens. Jude's first audience was probably familiar with the Book of Enoch.

Jude's brief quotation is not an endorsement of the Book of Enoch in any way. However, Jude affirms the truth of this specific prophecy. Writers of the Bible use original sources at times without certifying the books in which these sources originate. Divine inspiration guarantees the accuracy of such quotations, because ultimately God is speaking, not the human penman.

Enoch's prophecy previewed the glorious return of Christ to the earth with thousands upon thousands of His angels (v. 14). "Ten thousands" is an idiomatic way of referring to an unlimited number. Christ's return will be a glorious, spectacular event far beyond the limits of our full imaginations. He will come with all the glory and power that rightly belong to Him.

The prophecy makes it clear that no person can escape God's scrutiny (v. 15). The Lord will judge everyone when He returns, including all the ungodly. Jude uses the word "ungodly" four times to convey the false teachers are "irreverent" in character. It is no wonder that both their beliefs and their conduct, which flows from their beliefs, are ungodly.

After people believe that they are free from any scrutiny by God, they feel free to cut themselves loose from His standards (v. 15). They view God as a soft-hearted parent, for example, Who makes strong threats but cannot bring Himself to follow through on them. They conclude that God will not, therefore, act as He has said He will act and that God is unconcerned about how we live morally. The advocates of such a theology are in for a terrifying awakening when God Himself confronts them.

At His return the Lord will convict the ungodly with irrefutable evidence that their words and deeds are ungodly. In no way can our offensive words or acts be hidden from God (Hebrews 4:13).

16. Why do believers sometimes reflect false teachers in that they live as if God doesn't see or doesn't care about their hearts?

Murmurers and Complainers

Jude completes his denunciation of false teachers by bringing four final charges against them. First, they are grumblers and faultfinders who are vocally discontent. When a person is out of touch with God, he is bound to begin complaining about something (Jude 16).

17. Read Jude 16. Why is complaining sinful?

The ungodly complain about God and His ways because they have a critical spirit, for they are rebels at heart. For Christians to complain is an insult to God, Who graciously supplies us with all things.

Second, they lustfully follow their own self-centered cravings for what is forbidden morally (v. 16). They fault God for the way in which He runs things, because they have taken up with a new master, themselves. They have no sense of guilt as far as God's standards are concerned.

Third, they speak with over-swollen words about themselves (v. 16). They boast about themselves among those whom they wish to impress for their own selfish gain.

Fourth, they flatter others, using deceptive flattery (v. 16). They do this for their own advantage.

18. Why might a believer find him- or herself convicted by some of Jude's descriptions of false teachers?

In summary, false teachers put man in God's place, since they have no fear of God. When Christ returns, He will cut them down to size swiftly.

Making It Personal

19. Which of the descriptions of false teachers, if any, did you recognize as descriptive of your life?

20. What part might self-centeredness play in your thinking or acting like a false teacher?

21. Why would false teachers find it hard to gain access into a church known for encouraging words, honesty, selflessness, and service?

22. Which of these descriptions describe your church?

23. What can you do to contribute toward making your church less reflective of false teachers?

24. Memorize Jude 10.

Distinctive Christian Living

Christians are to live distinctive lives.

Jude 17–25

"But ye, beloved, building up yourselves on your most holy faith, praying in the Holy Ghost, keep yourselves in the love of God, looking for the mercy of our Lord Jesus Christ unto eternal life" (Jude 20, 21).

The fact that everyone has unique fingerprints has long been established, though no one could know this absolutely for sure unless all the fingerprints of everyone who has ever lived were gathered and compared. Those who have arching fingerprints have the rarest type. Arching fingerprints have lines that move across the finger with no lines doubling back to the same side. Only five percent of the world's population has arching fingerprints. Not good news for criminals who happen to have arching fingerprints!

Getting Started

1. What three characteristics make you distinctively you?

2. What would you list as three distinctions of a believer?

Today's lesson focuses attention on the believer faced with living in the last days. Jude urges the believer to endeavor to live a distinctive Christian life in the face of profoundly unchristian false religionists.

Searching the Scriptures

Last-time mockers

Jude's "beloved" reference to his readers makes the transition from his burning denouncement of the false teachers to his exhortation on Christian living. Repetition is a good teaching tool. While Jude provides information on apostasy, his first readers have also the warning of the apostles.

3. Read Acts 20:29, 30. What did Paul call false teachers?

4. What did he warn the believers about the false teachers' actions?

The apostles predicted that mockers of the truth would appear in the last time (Jude 18). The "last time" is the period of time between Christ's two advents. This time is upon us now. Apostates scoff at God's truth and advocate a belief and lifestyle that is self-centered and sinful.

Causing Division

These mockers promote division by making distinctions between their own views and the faith believers have been taught (vv. 3, 4). In this way they separate themselves and their followers from others. A spirit of elitism characterizes them as mockers of God's truth.

5. Read 1 Peter 5:5–7. What important truths did the false teachers ignore?

6. Why is pride so offensive to God?

The arrogance of the false teachers has a fatal flaw. They are estranged from the Holy Spirit so that their thoughts are driven and controlled by their carnal appetites and desires.

Building and Praying

Jude draws a crucial contrast between believers and apostate mockers of God. In his contrast he presents Christian living that is distinctive of the faith.

First, Jude exhorts believers to personal edification (Jude 20). We are to build up ourselves on God's truth, which is the faith that has been entrusted to us (v. 3).

7. Read Jude 20. In the world's estimation, what does it mean for a person to build him- or herself up?

8. How is building yourself up in the faith different from the world's understanding of building yourself up?

The idea of "building up" is that of finishing a structure for which the foundation has already been laid. This is a lifelong activity.

The faith upon which we grow has been set apart for our benefit through the inspiration of the Holy Spirit (2 Timothy 3:16). It is unique in the message that it teaches and in the moral transformation it produces in those who embrace it by faith (Jude 20). We are building up ourselves as we mature spiritually through studying, believing, and obeying the Scriptures (2 Timothy 2:15). A correct understanding of Biblical doctrine is the starting point. When our obedience and commitment to God's truth follows, a godly character is under construction.

9. What are some general areas in which a believer needs to be built up in the faith?

Second, Jude instructs believers to pray in the Holy Spirit (Jude 20). This is praying according to the Spirit's directions and inner prompting" (Ephesians 5:18).

A Christian's prayer life can become mechanical and mundane. Jude's exhortation calls us to involve ourselves actively in prayer. As we approach God in openness and dependence upon Him, the Holy Spirit guides and prompts us in forming our prayers. We can know the Holy Spirit prompts us only to obedience to God and to involvement in His will.

10. What part does Bible study play in helping a believer develop an effective prayer life?

Obeying and Looking

Third, Jude urges believers to cultivate the love relationship that they have with Christ (Jude 21). This is also what Jesus is telling us to do in John 15:9 and 10, when He speaks of abiding in His love by obeying His commandments.

Jude is not instructing us on how to keep our personal salvation. Our salvation does not depend on personal effort. If that were true,

Jude would be teaching legalism, which substitutes works for God's grace. Jude assures believers of their security in Christ (Jude 24). Our obedience to Christ is an expression of our love to Him. We obey because we love Him Who first loved us and saved us (1 John 4:19).

11. How do our works change when we do them as a response to Christ's love instead of as a way to gain His favor?

Fourth, Jude exhorts us to look for Christ's return (Jude 21). The fact that His coming for the church could occur at any moment makes Jude's exhortation all the more imperative. The false teachers try to kill this hope by scoffing at the idea of God's breaking into human history in a miraculous and dramatic way (2 Peter 3:4).

12. What could you do as a daily reminder of Christ's any moment return?

Christ's return for us will be a merciful act on His part (Jude 21). With the transformation of the bodies in which we now live, our redemption will be complete at last. We received God's mercy when He saved us and we need it day by day. His mercy will be needed at the last, and Jude reassures us that we will receive it at Christ's return.

Eternal life is also ours now (v. 21). We have passed from spiritual death to eternal life (John 5:24). With our transfer from earth to Heaven at Christ's return, we will begin to experience eternal life in His presence. Jude exhorts us with good reason to watch expectantly for Christ's return.

Rescuing Others

Fifth, Jude exhorts us to become involved in the often painful work of rescuing those who come under the devastating influence of false doctrine. The context of this exhortation for rescue operations is the existing threat of false teachers to the assembly of believers.

13. What excuses might believers give for ignoring those who are beginning to come under the influence of a false teacher?

Three groups of believers need the compassion of other believers (Jude 22, 23). Jude's admonition for believers to be involved in these three rescue missions fits with New Testament instructions.

14. Read Galatians 6:1, 2. What qualification does Paul give for those who seek to restore an erring brother or sister in Christ?

15. Why is that qualification important?

The first group is those who doubt (Jude 22). They are wavering in their trust in God's Word. The word "difference" suggests that a person is uncertain about what he has been taught. The false teachers' teaching and lifestyle have resulted in uncertainty about the faith. When a Christian flirts with false doctrine and begins to waver in his confidence in the faith, he needs help. He has begun to assent in his thinking to erroneous doctrine while questioning the true.

Those who doubt need the compassion of those who know God's Word and are convinced of its truthfulness (v. 22). The zeal for purity in the assembly of believers should not be such that those who would have questions and misunderstandings could not express them. It should not be difficult for them to find a fellow-believer who will sit and listen and talk things through.

16. What could your church do to help identify those who have serious questions about what the Bible teaches?

We should be merciful to doubters as the objects of God's mercy, even as we all are. We cannot be soft on Biblical doctrine, but to those who have questions we must always demonstrate patient understanding.

17. Why might a believer criticize another believer for having doubts about the truth?

The second group are those who are about to fall into the flames of God's judgment (v. 23). They see no reason not to entertain false doctrine in their thinking and to engage in the lifestyle that accompanies it. The new lifestyle is quite comfortable, and it liberates from the old ways that restrict satisfying one's own desires.

Jude implies the need for drastic action by stating that the rescuer needs to deliver the person from falling into the fire. False teachers are apostates, and apostates are unsaved. The doubters who persist in following their erroneous doctrines and practices will end up with them in the dismal abyss of divine judgment. Their fall will evidence that they were unsaved counterfeits. Jude calls us to snatch them from plunging into the flames of eternal judgment, like we would snatch brands from a fire.

The final group is described as wearing clothing "spotted by the flesh" (v. 23). This figure of speech means they are stained by immoral physical activities. Our compassion for them is to be mixed with fear, however. We cannot let their moral infection spread to us. The rescue is to be carried out with a hatred of the contamination that sin brings.

Those who have fallen must, in their repentance, discard the corrupting effect of impurity (v. 23). We must expect a complete change of their attitude toward the truth and a reversal of their lifestyle.

Kept from Falling

Christians live with the constant pressure to stumble into doctrinal and moral error. God is on guard, however (v. 24). He protects us against the apostate mockers with all their doctrinal deceptions that produce deadly dangers and pitfalls. God uses His Word, such as Jude's letter, with its insights and warnings to steer us away from a fatal fall. Believer's rescue missions are another means by which God restores His people who would carelessly dabble in false teaching.

18. In your estimation are rescue missions to save erring brothers and sisters in Christ being conducted as often as they should be conducted today? Explain.

God will ultimately usher all of us into His immediate presence (v. 24). We will be presented "faultless." The word was used of sacrificial animals offered to God that bore no physical spot or blemish. We will be without blame because of Christ's sacrificial death, which makes us acceptable before God.

God's Attributes

Jude praises God and recognizes four of God's eternal attributes (v. 25). His glory is the sum of all that He is. His majesty is His transcendent greatness over all of His creation. His dominion is His absolute sovereignty over the universe. And His power is His total freedom to act according to His will.

19. How could you practice the celebration of God as part of your distinctive Christian living?

Making It Personal

20. Which of the distinctions of a Christian are most evident in your life?

21. Which of the distinctions do you need to allow God to develop further in your life?

22. What impact did the Bible books you studied in this course have on your life?

23. What are two or three major courses of action you need to take as a result of studying these books?

24. Memorize Jude 20 and 21